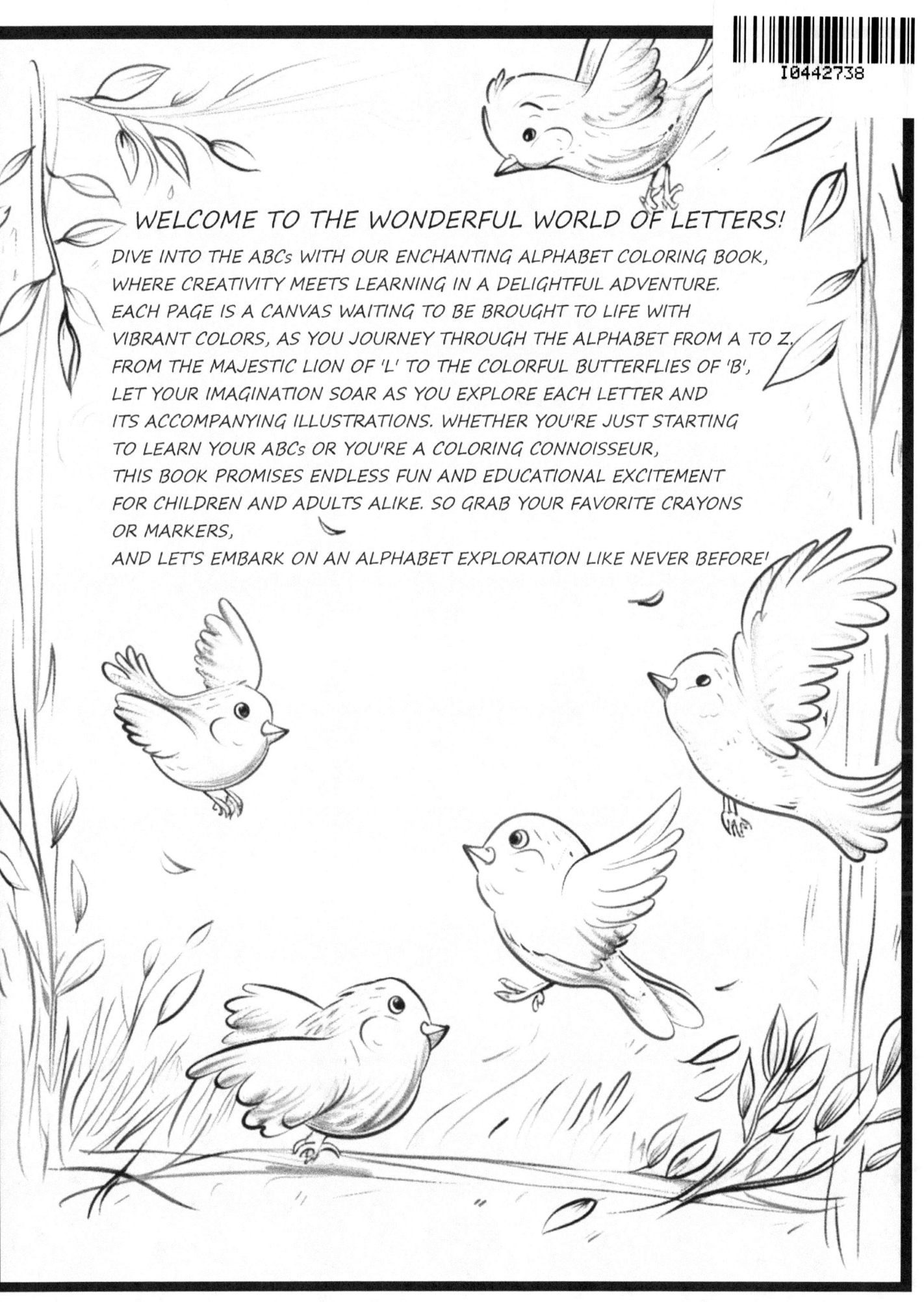

WELCOME TO THE WONDERFUL WORLD OF LETTERS!

DIVE INTO THE ABCs WITH OUR ENCHANTING ALPHABET COLORING BOOK, WHERE CREATIVITY MEETS LEARNING IN A DELIGHTFUL ADVENTURE. EACH PAGE IS A CANVAS WAITING TO BE BROUGHT TO LIFE WITH VIBRANT COLORS, AS YOU JOURNEY THROUGH THE ALPHABET FROM A TO Z. FROM THE MAJESTIC LION OF 'L' TO THE COLORFUL BUTTERFLIES OF 'B', LET YOUR IMAGINATION SOAR AS YOU EXPLORE EACH LETTER AND ITS ACCOMPANYING ILLUSTRATIONS. WHETHER YOU'RE JUST STARTING TO LEARN YOUR ABCs OR YOU'RE A COLORING CONNOISSEUR, THIS BOOK PROMISES ENDLESS FUN AND EDUCATIONAL EXCITEMENT FOR CHILDREN AND ADULTS ALIKE. SO GRAB YOUR FAVORITE CRAYONS OR MARKERS, AND LET'S EMBARK ON AN ALPHABET EXPLORATION LIKE NEVER BEFORE!

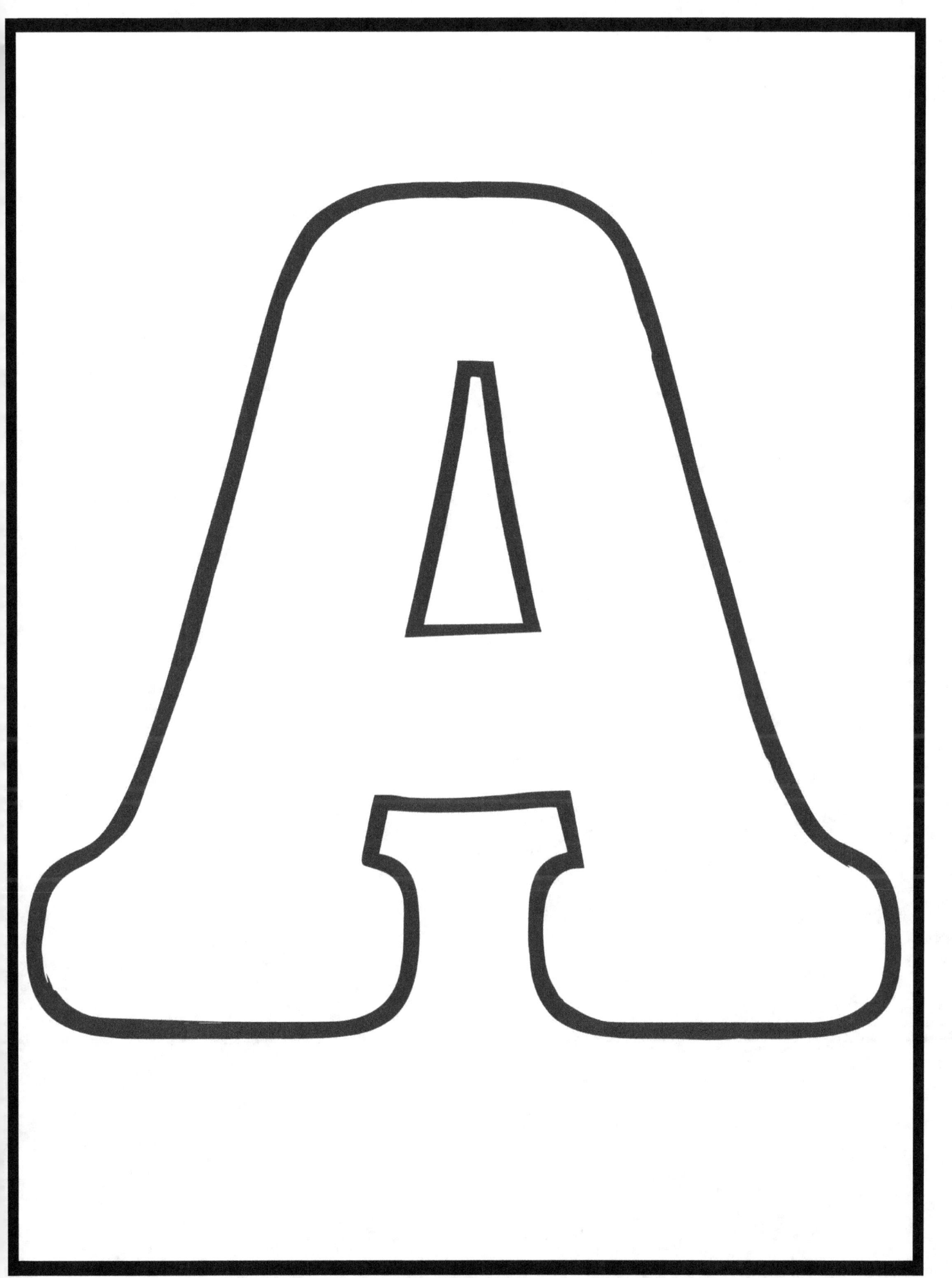

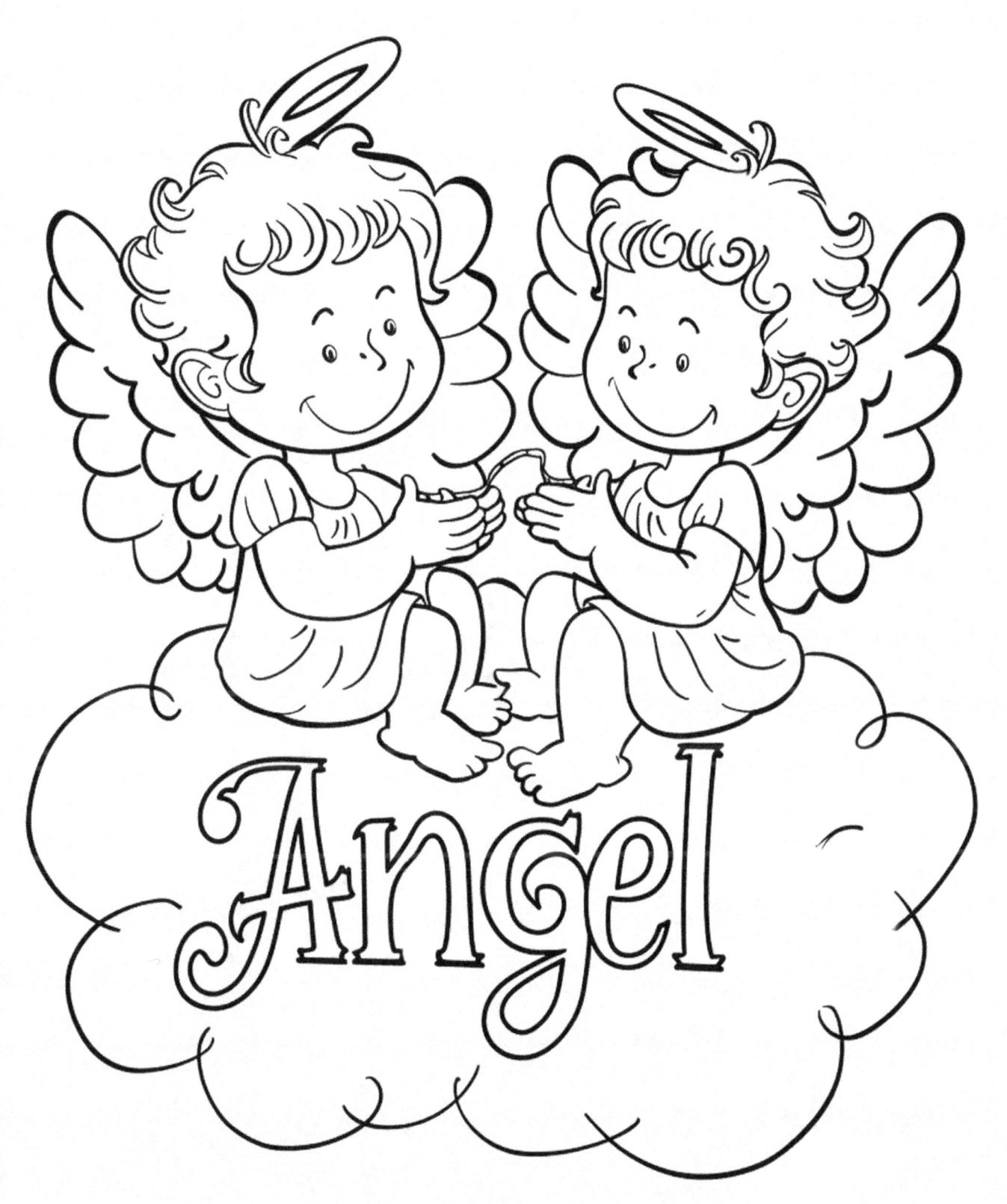

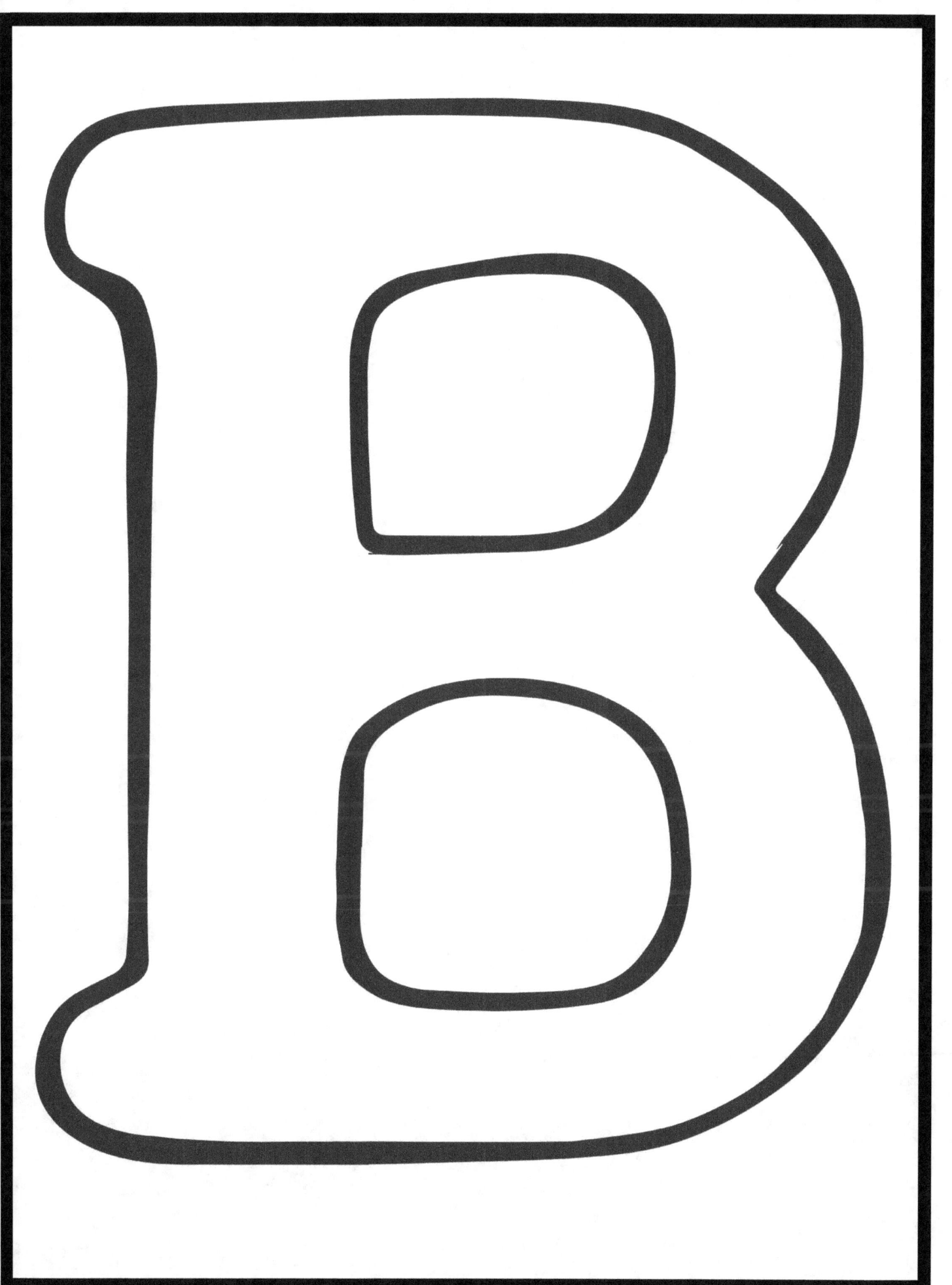

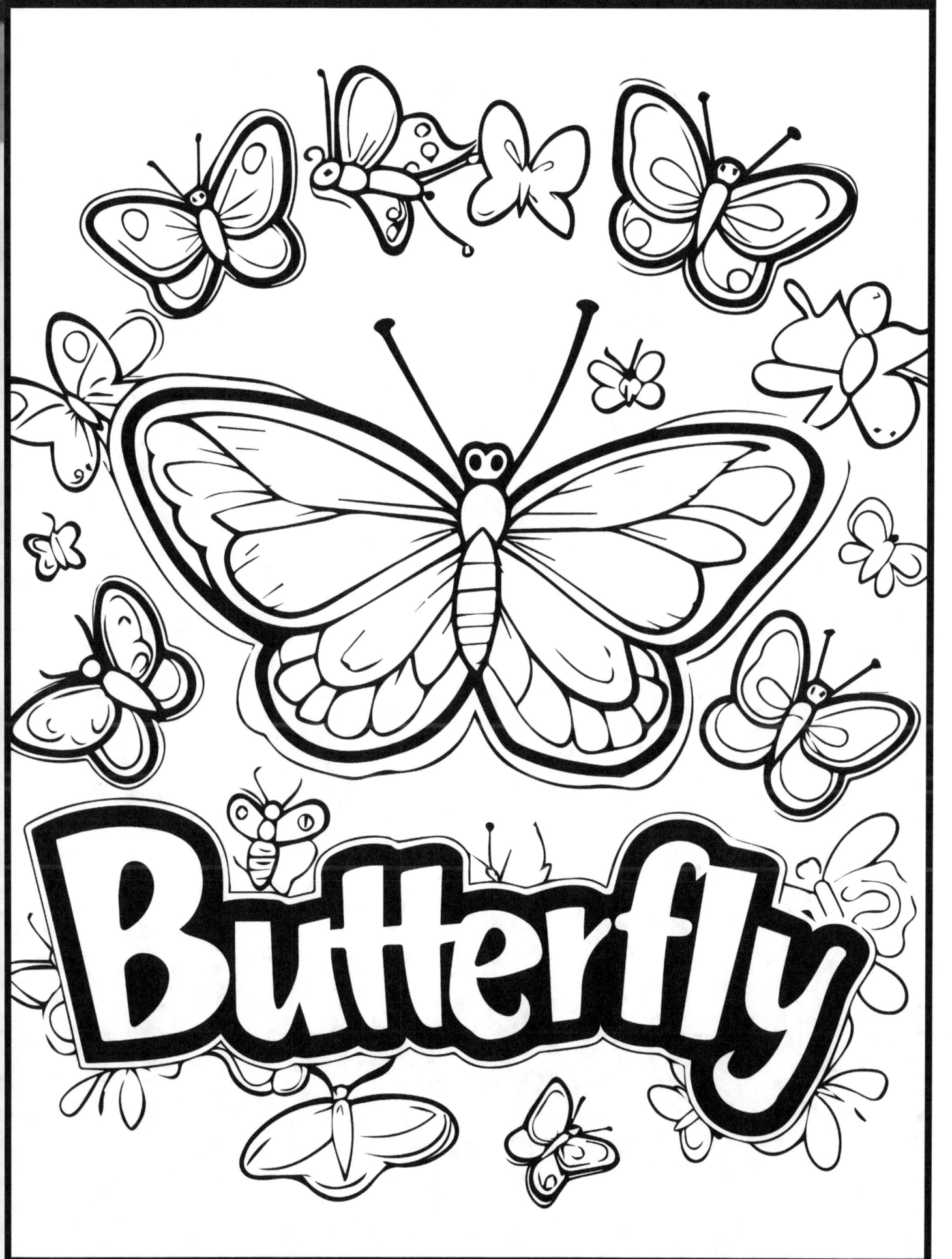

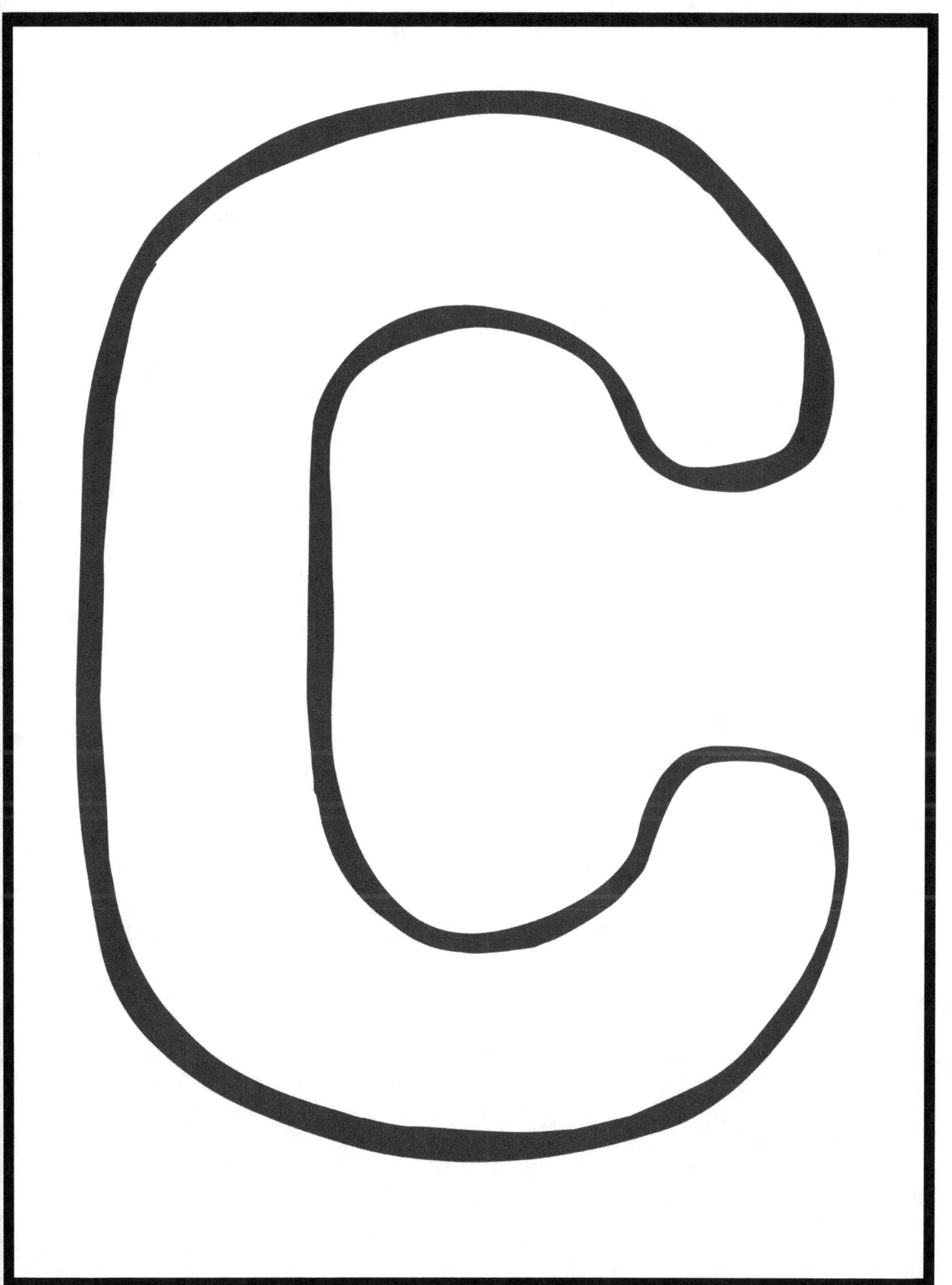

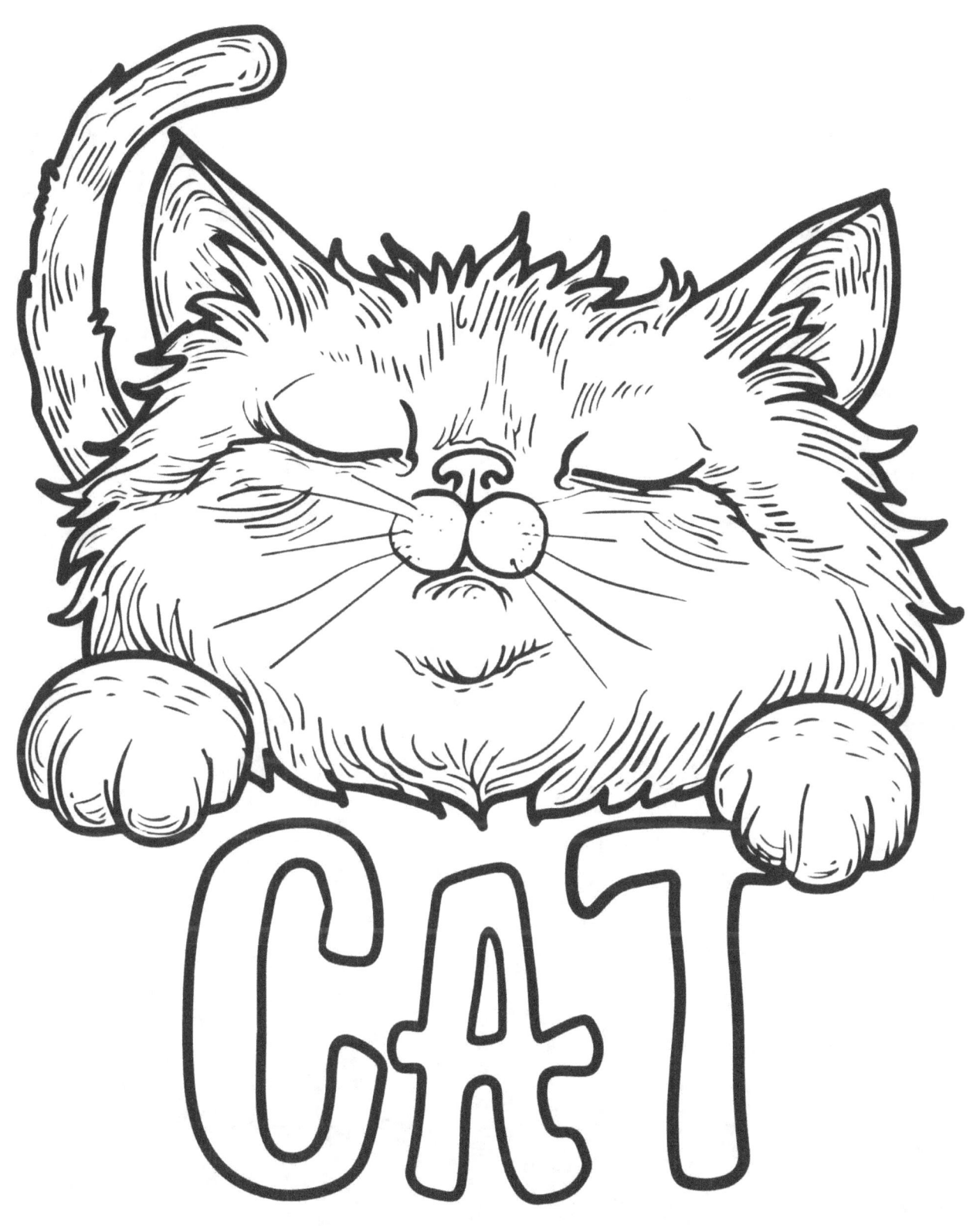

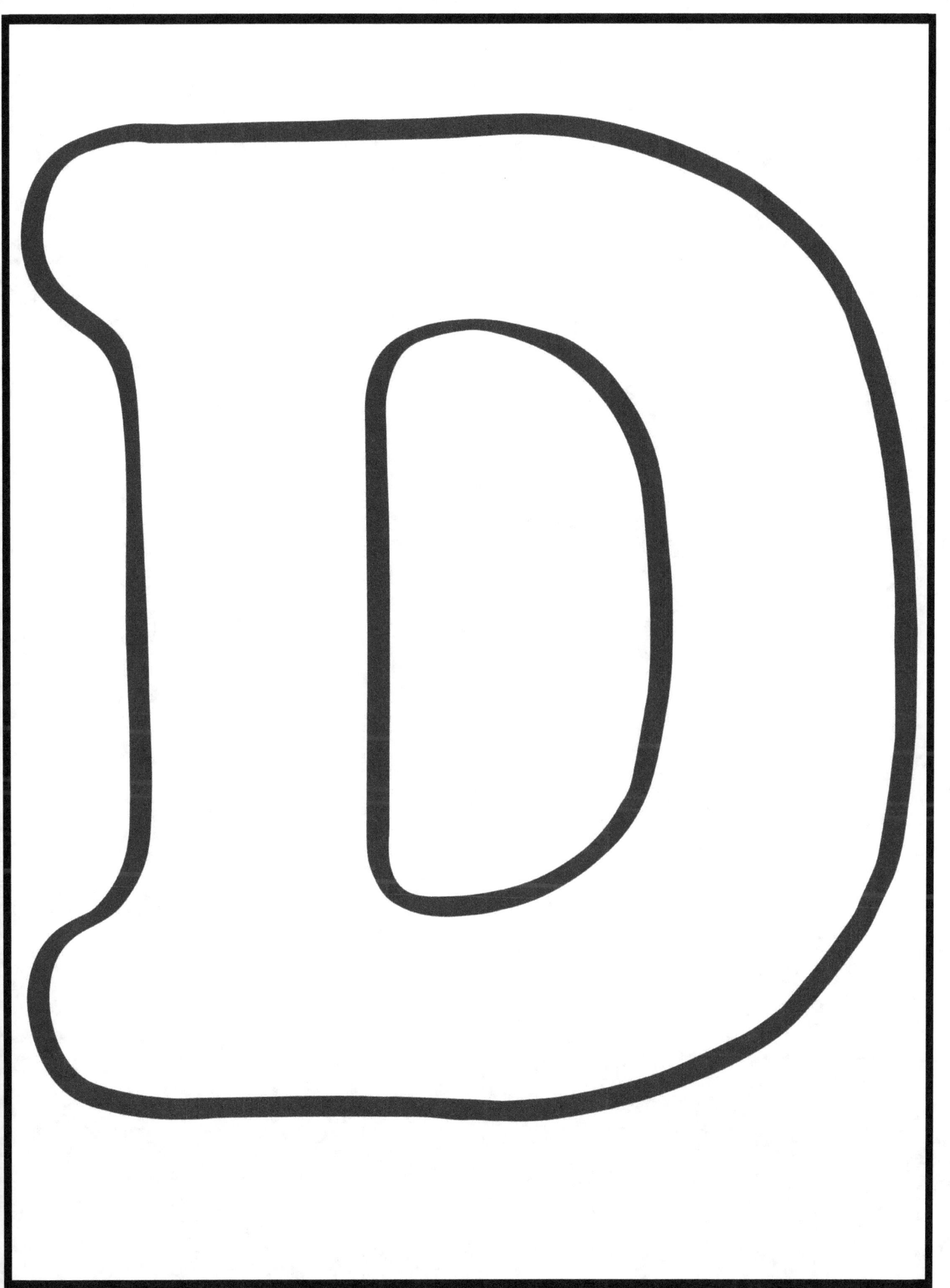

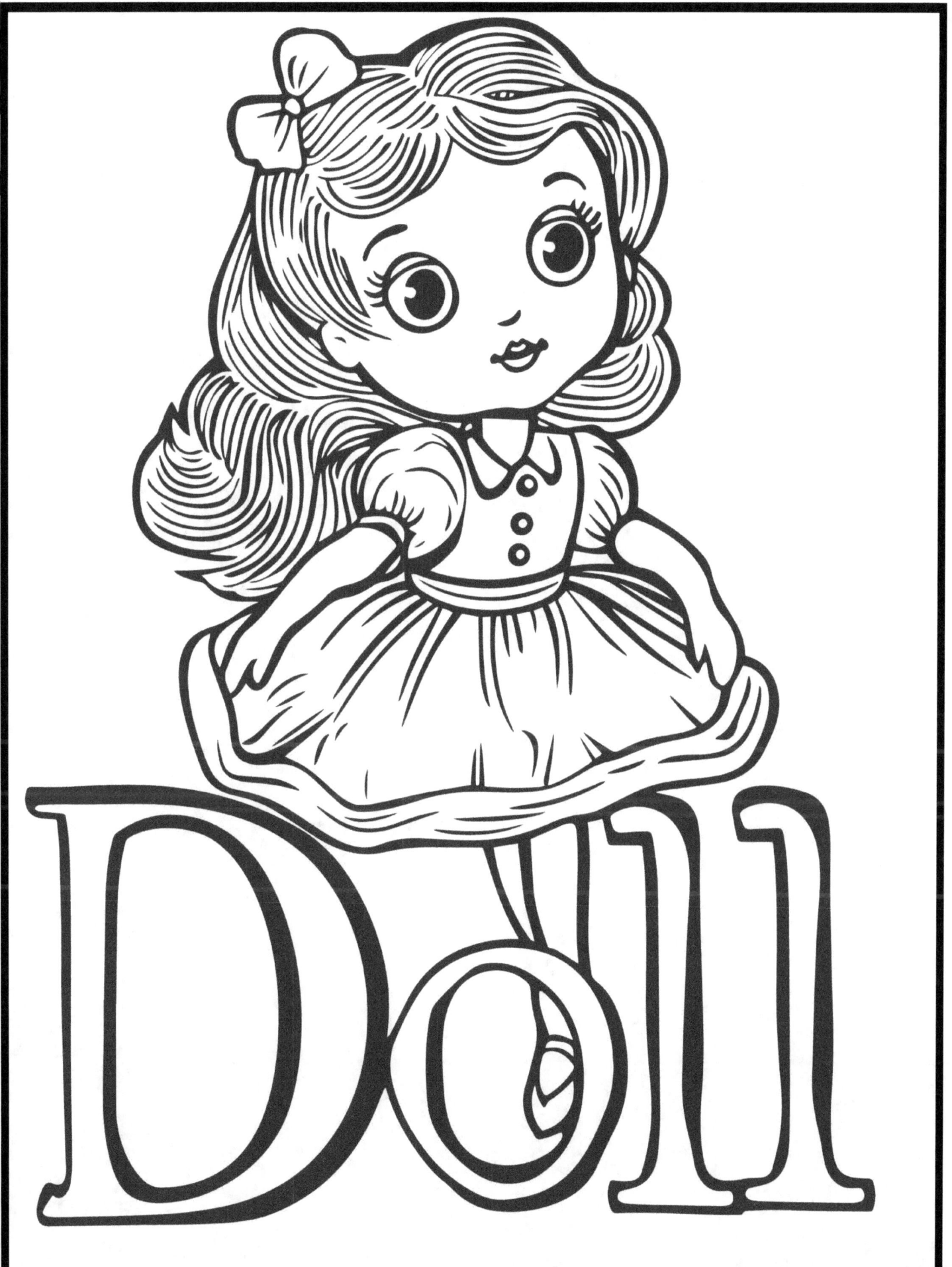

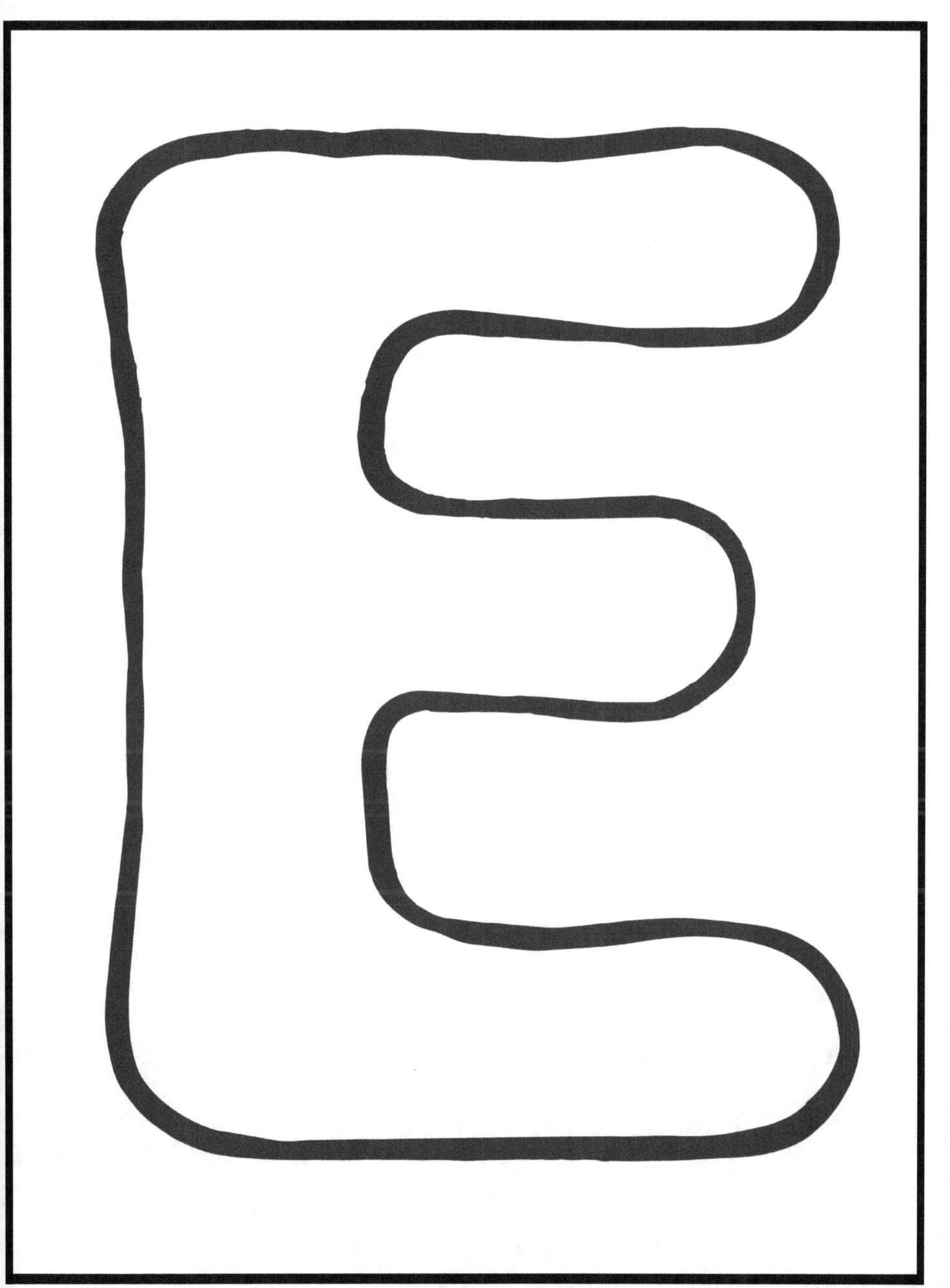

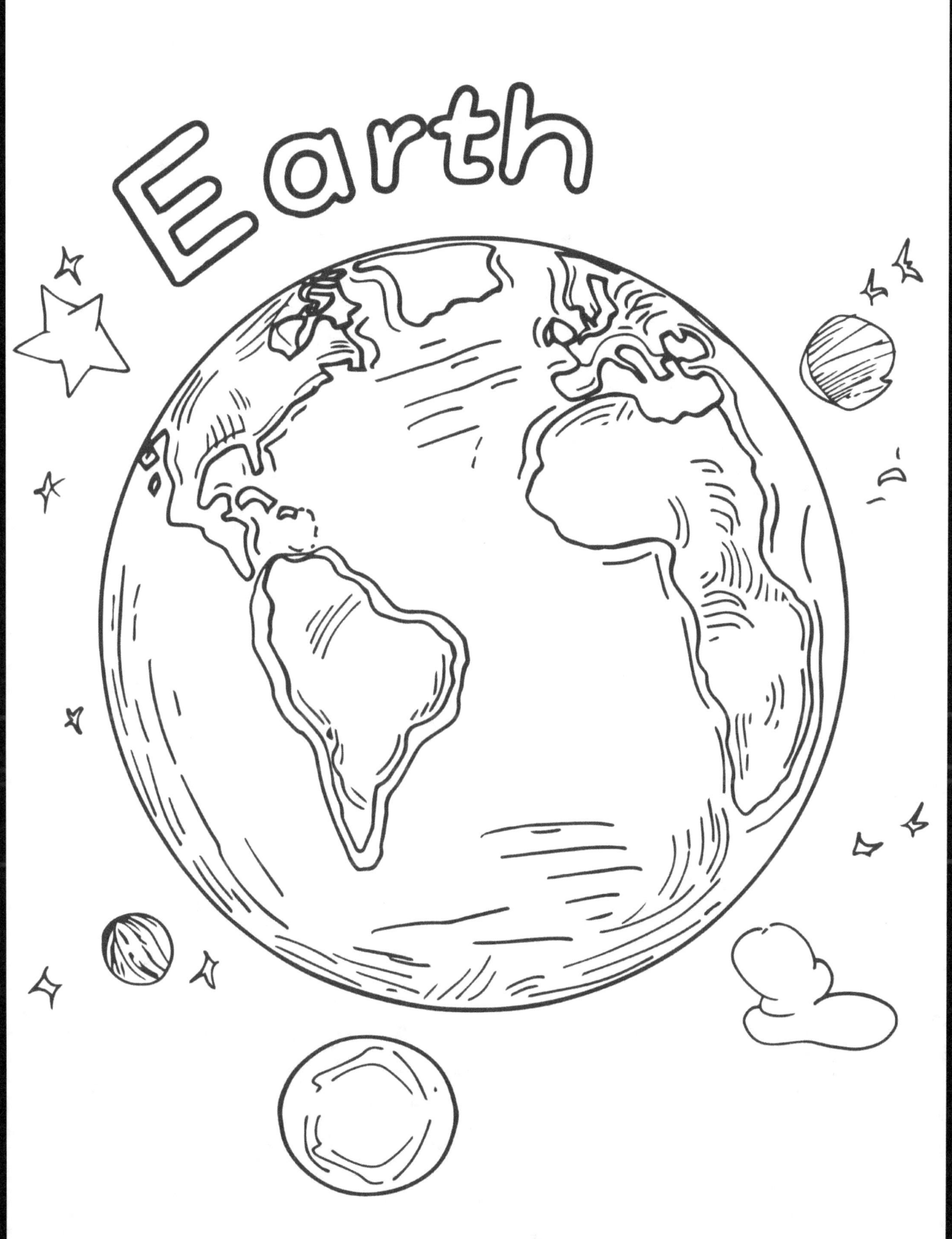

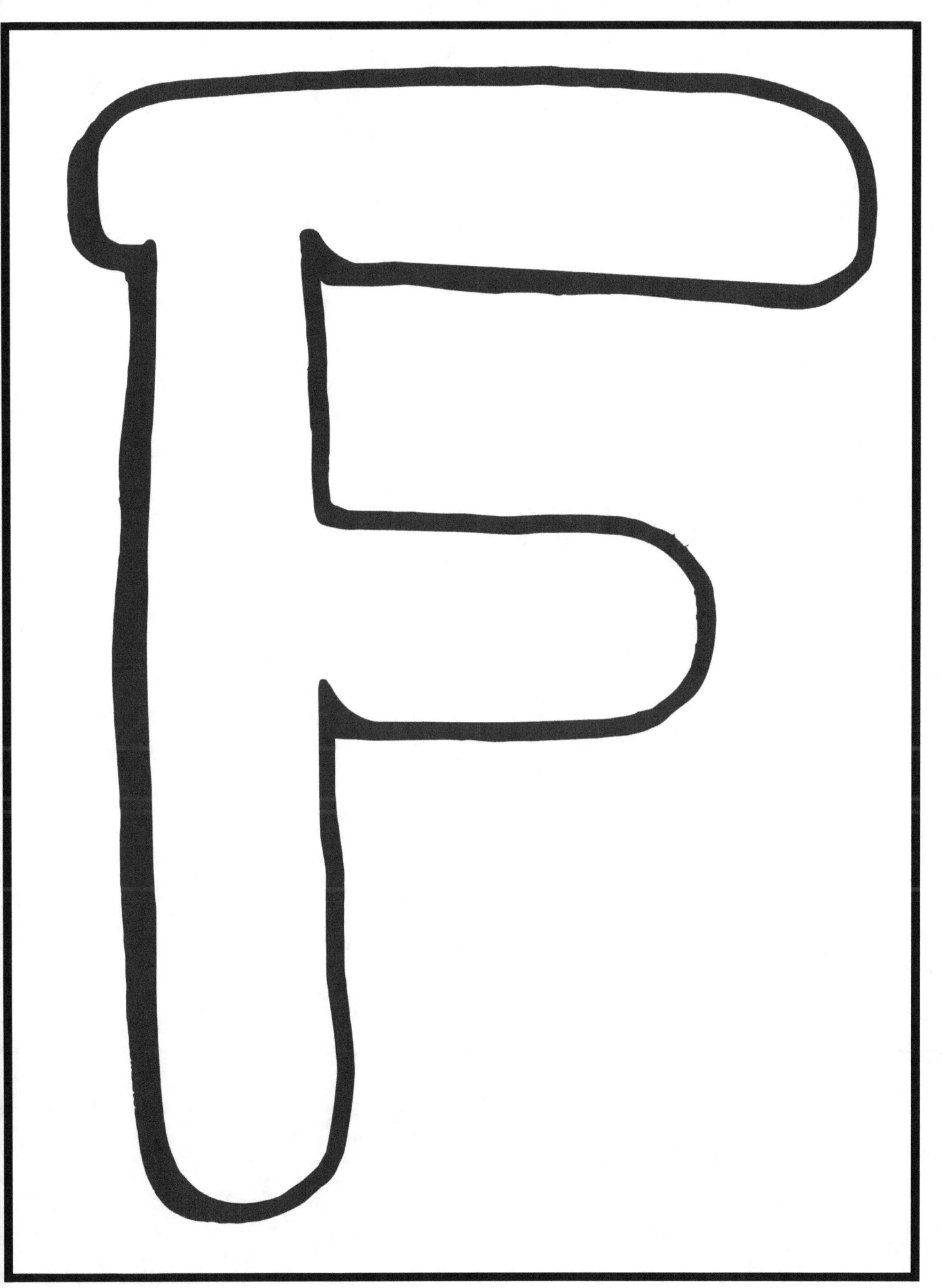

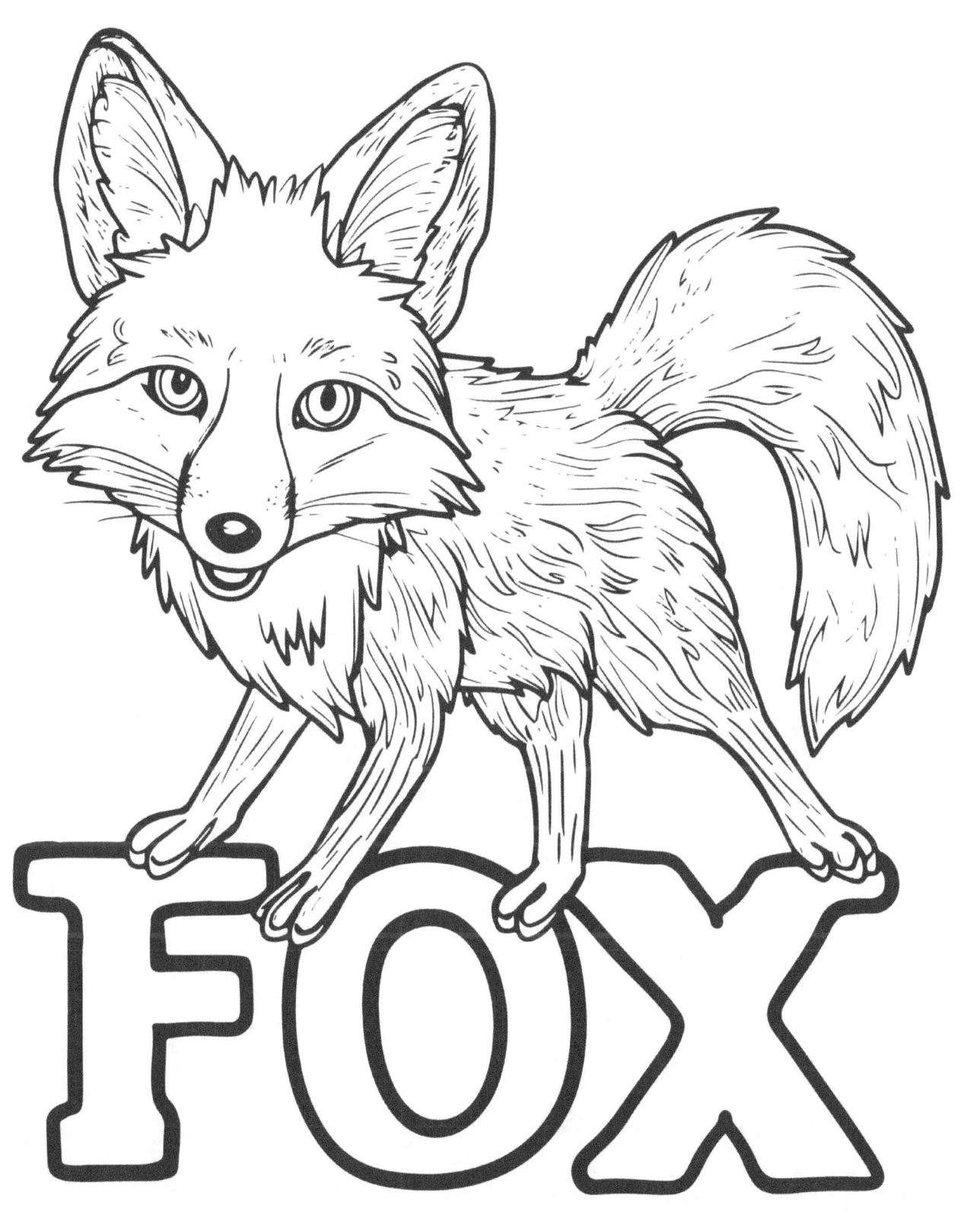

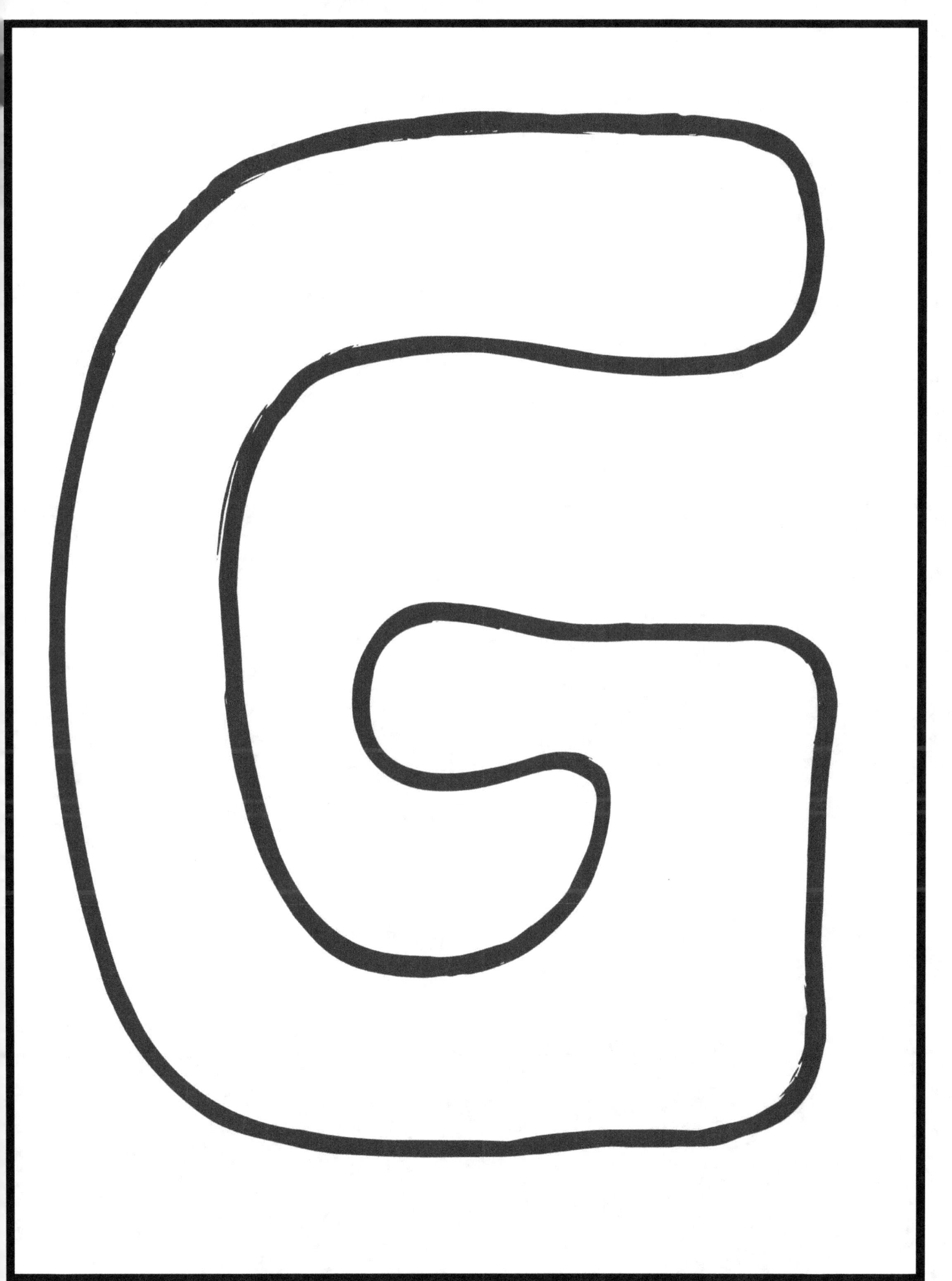

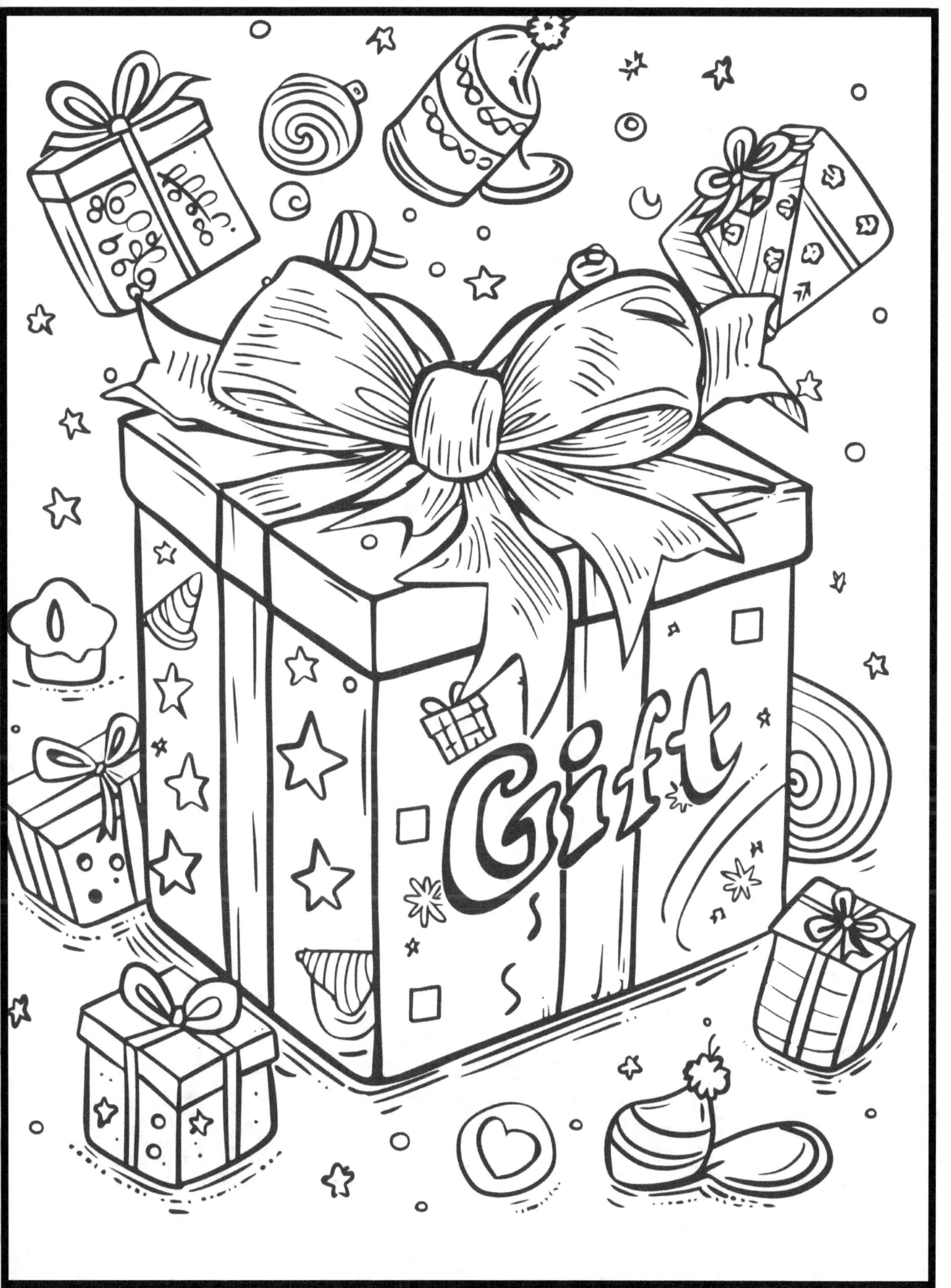

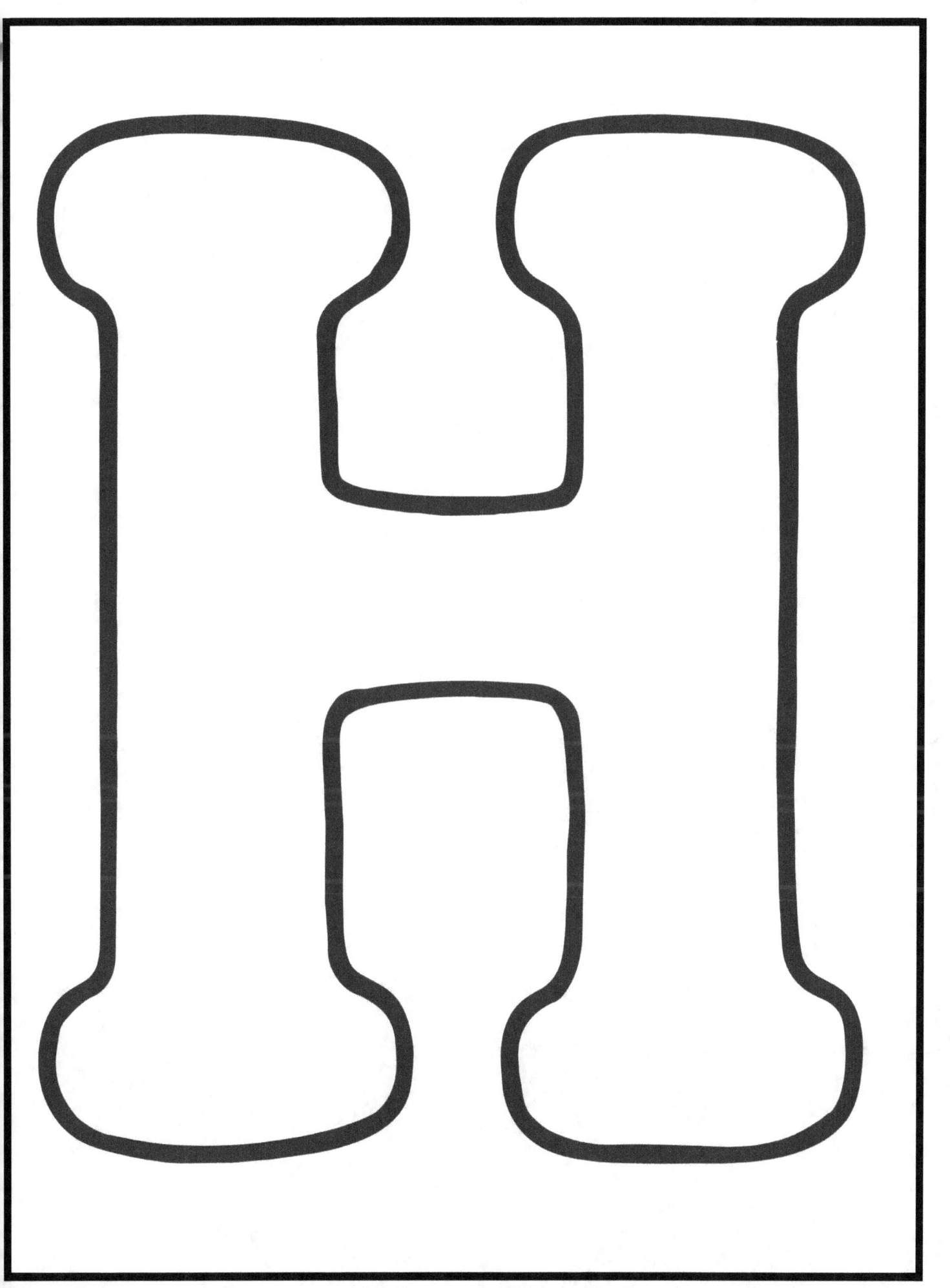

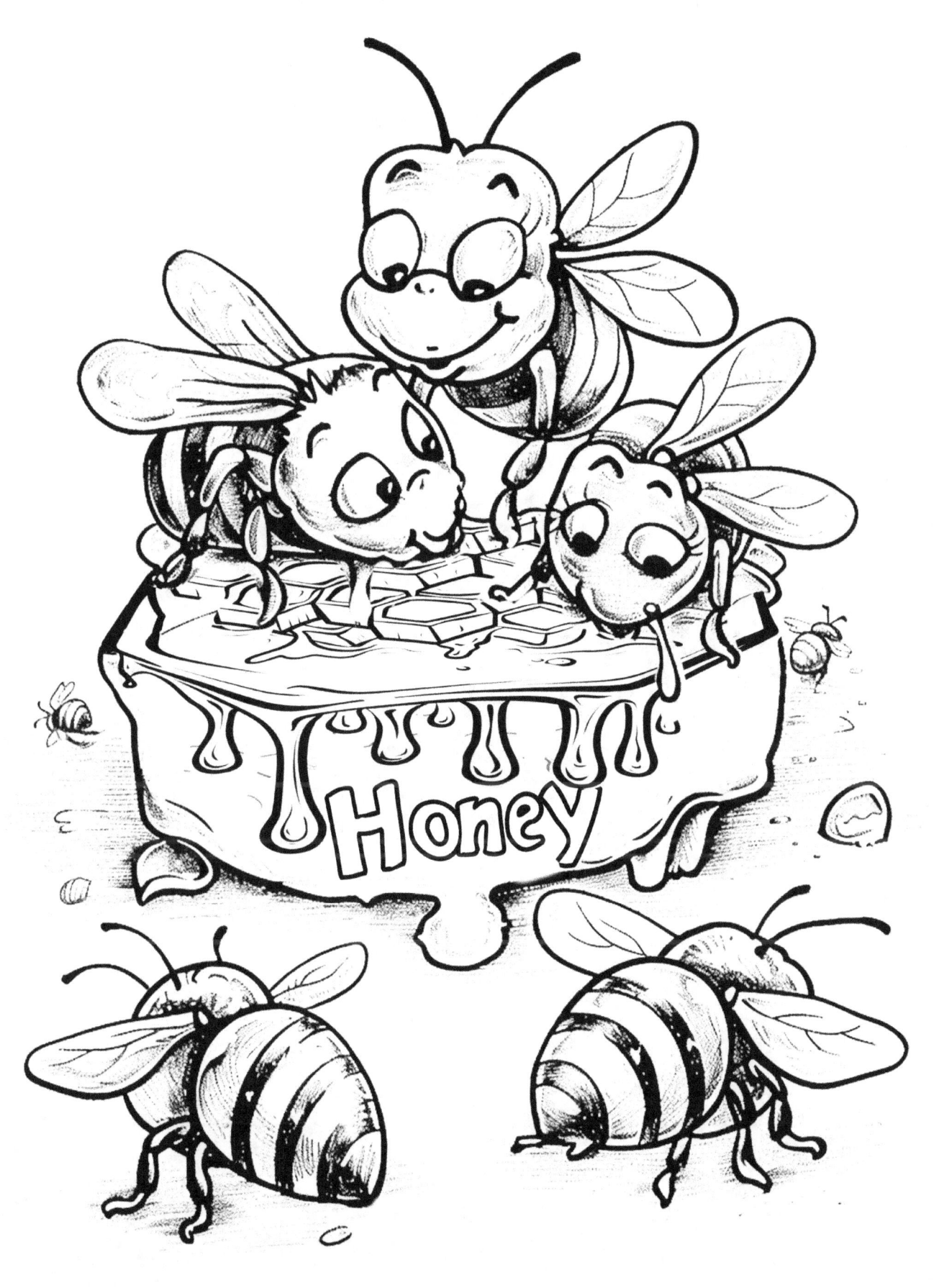

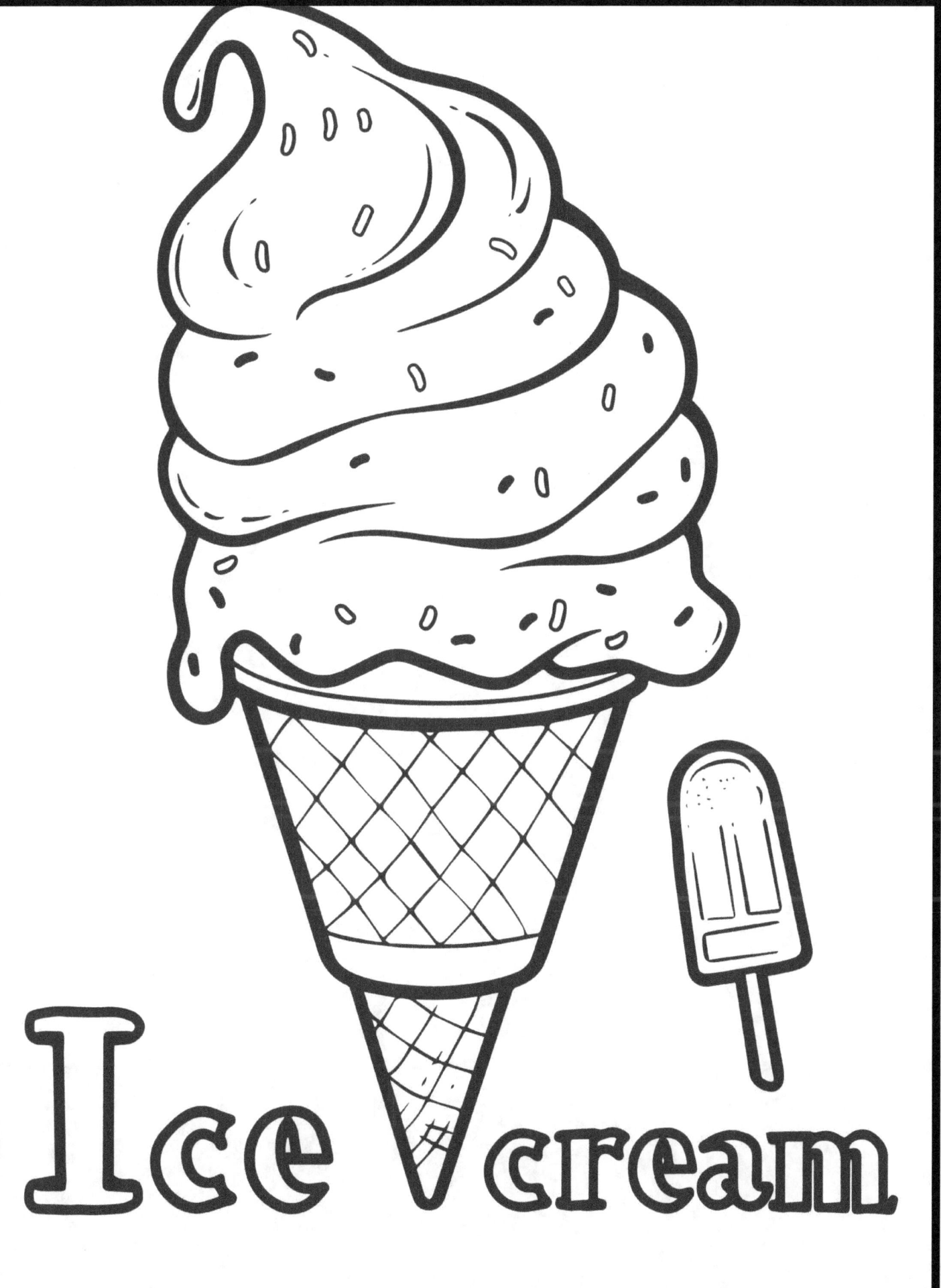

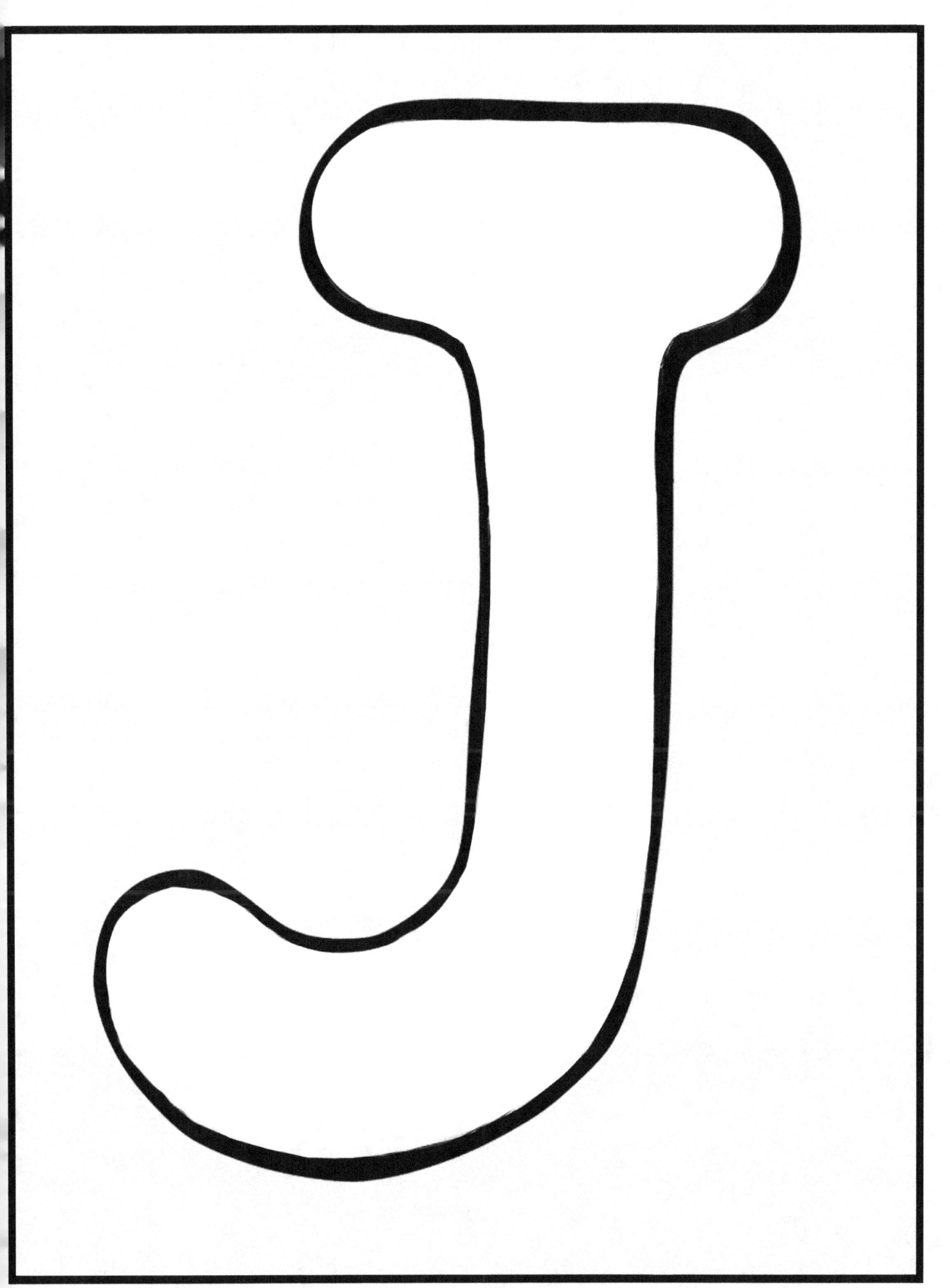

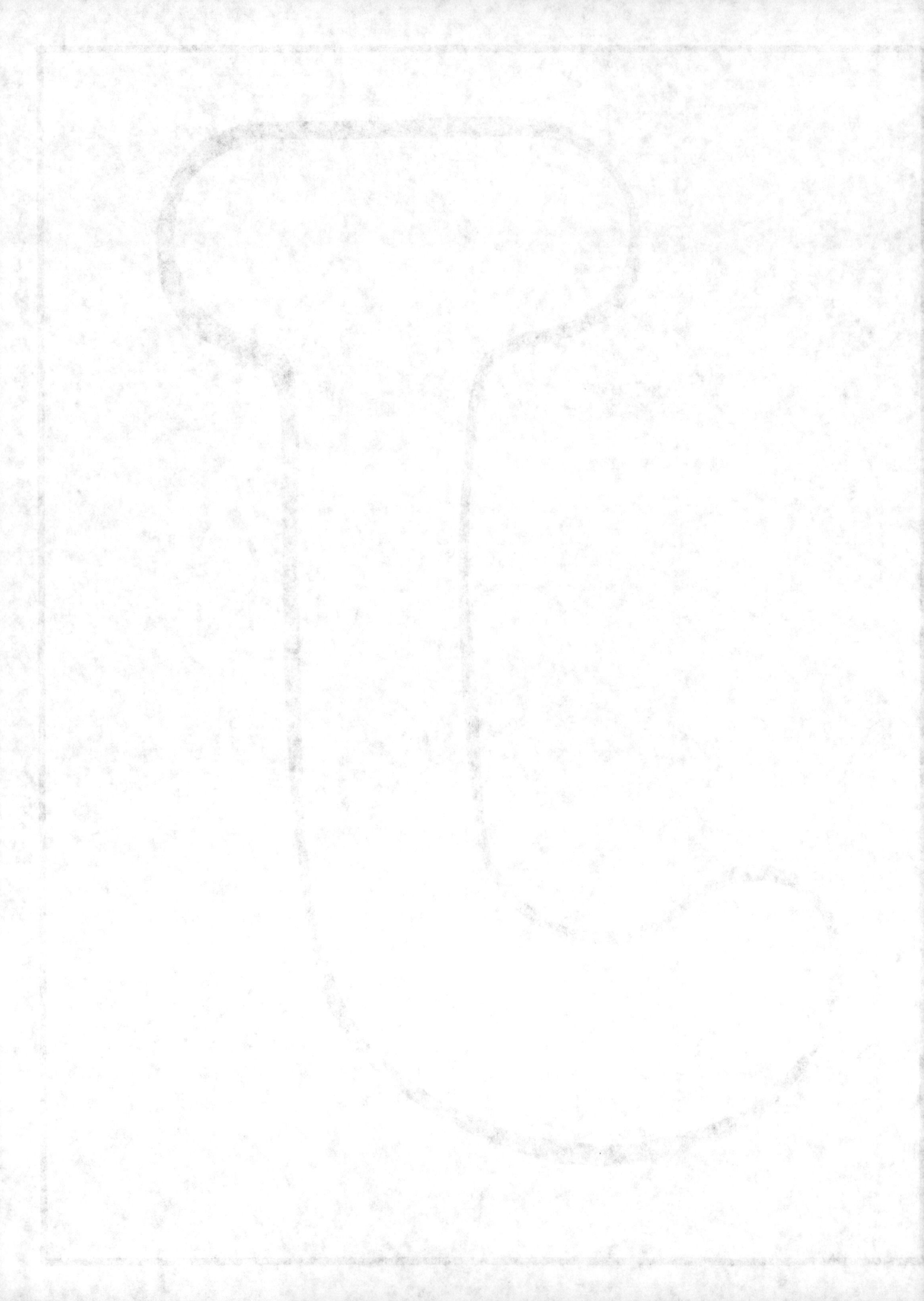

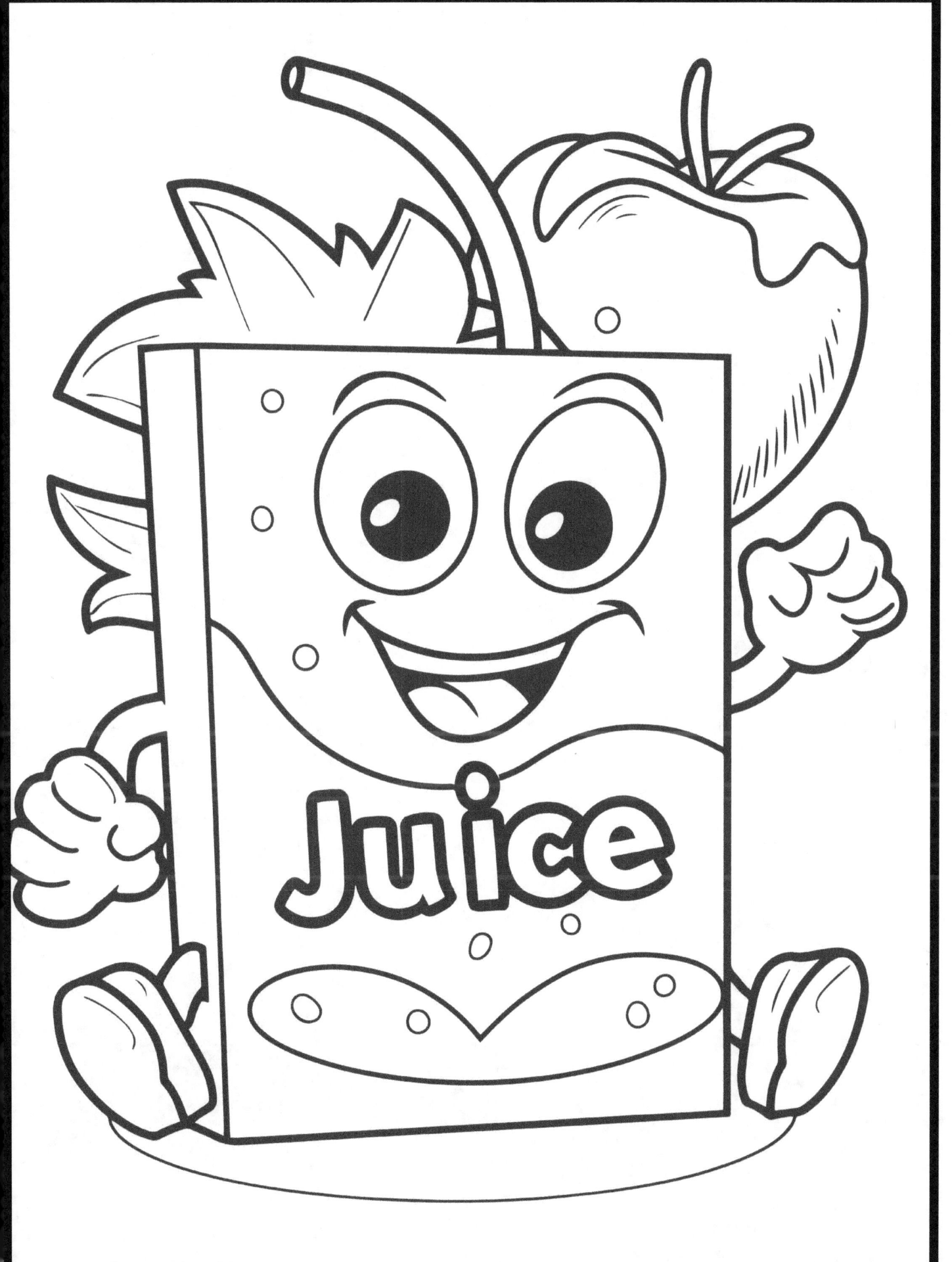

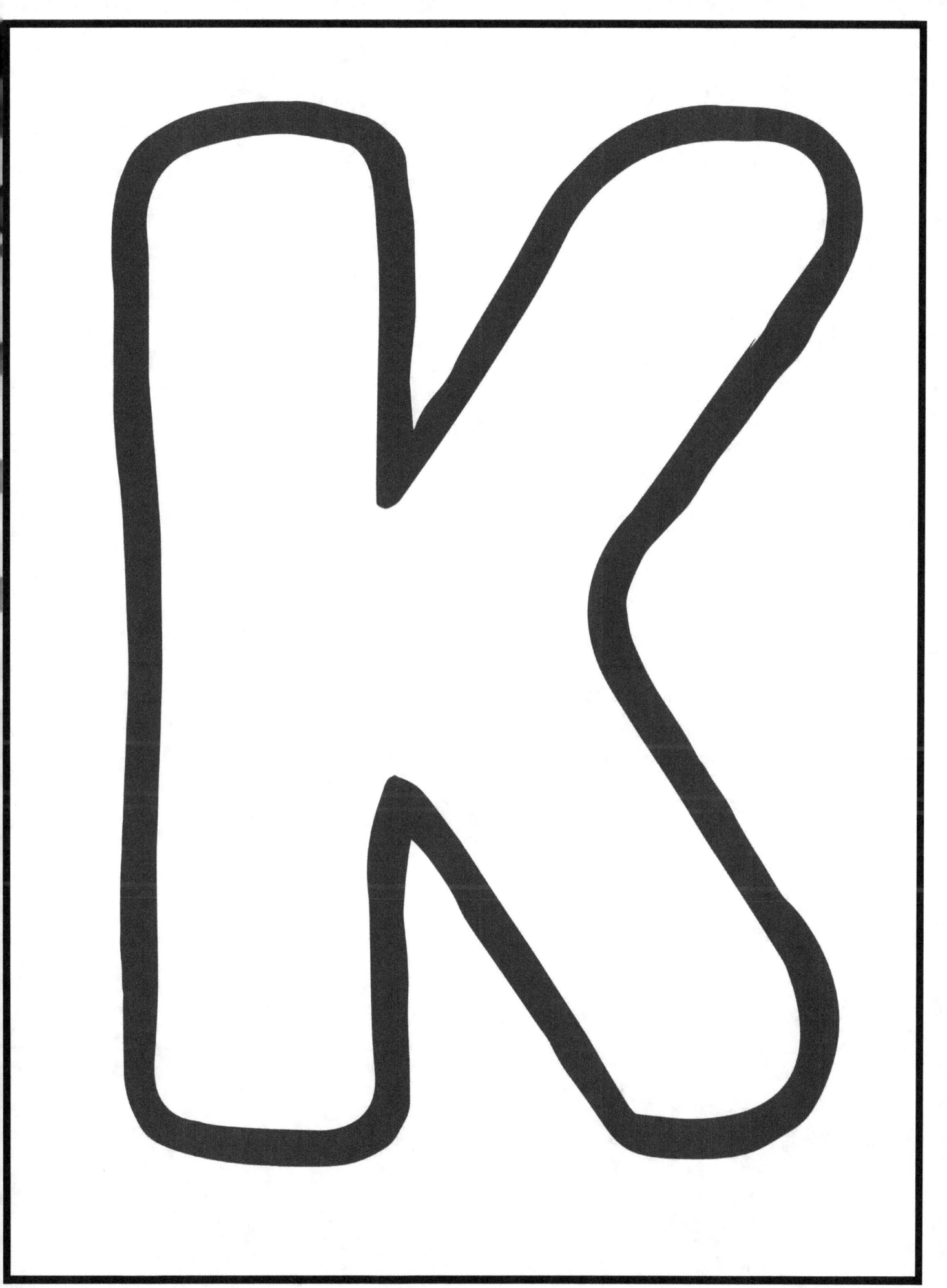

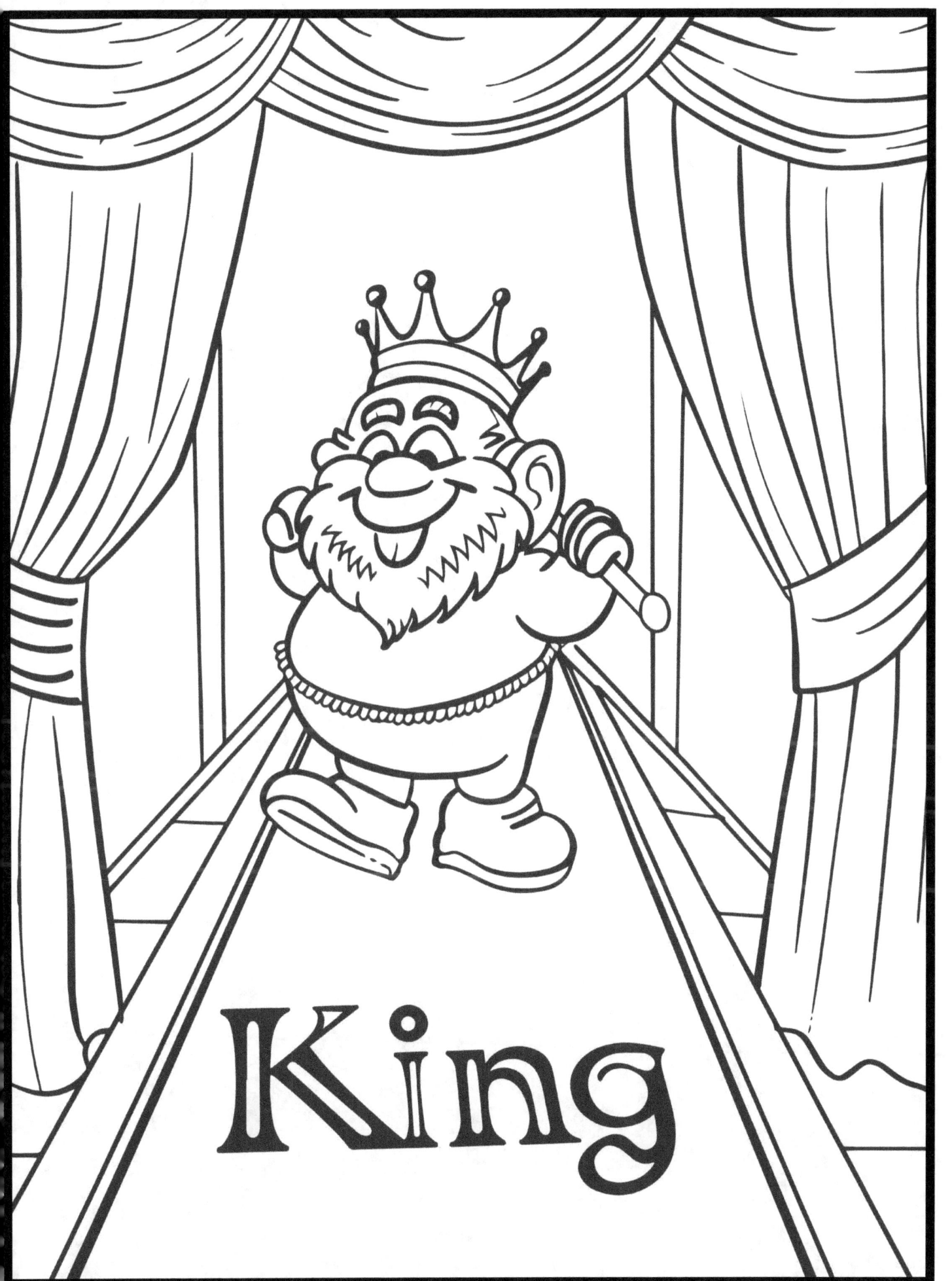

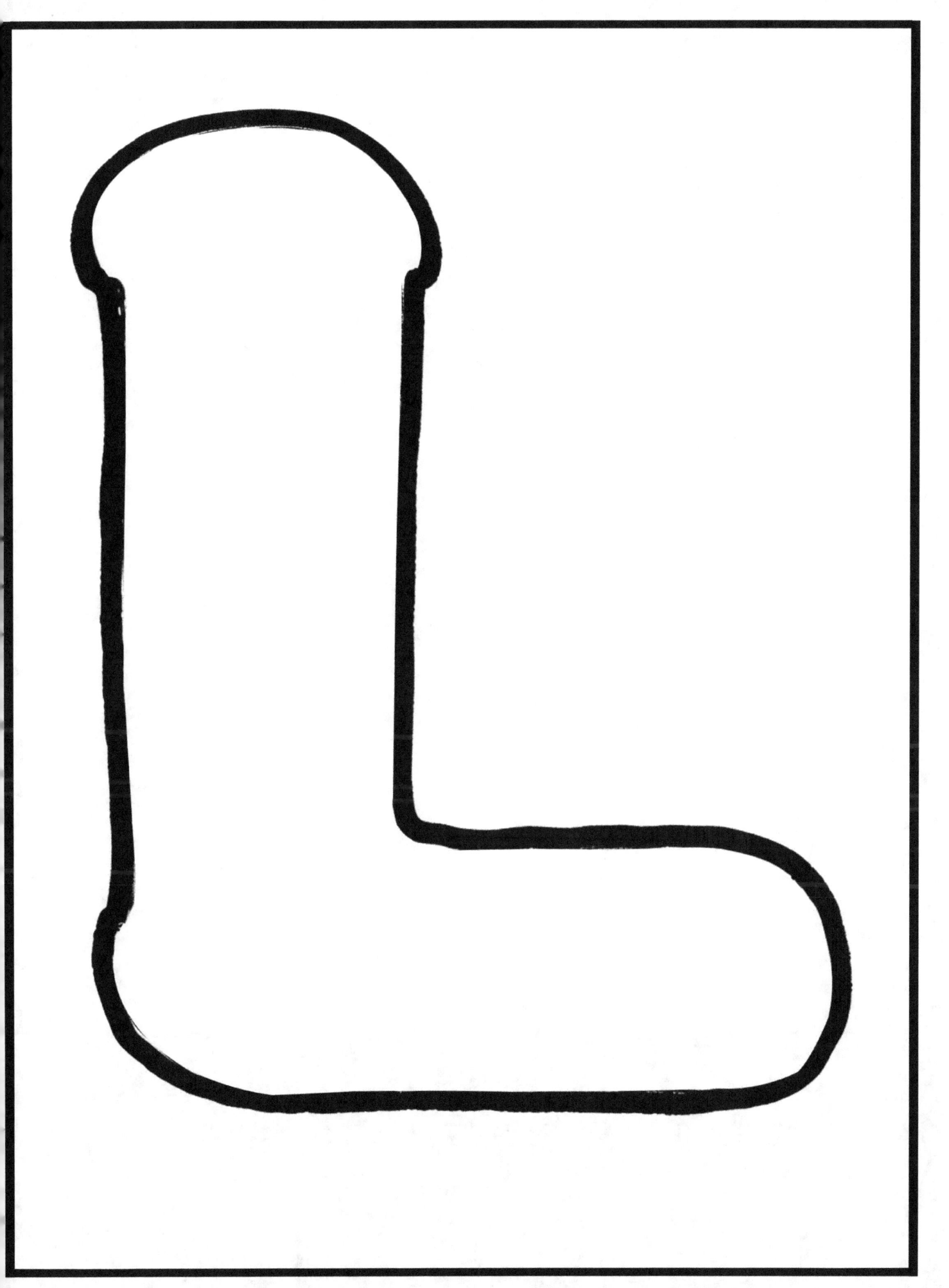

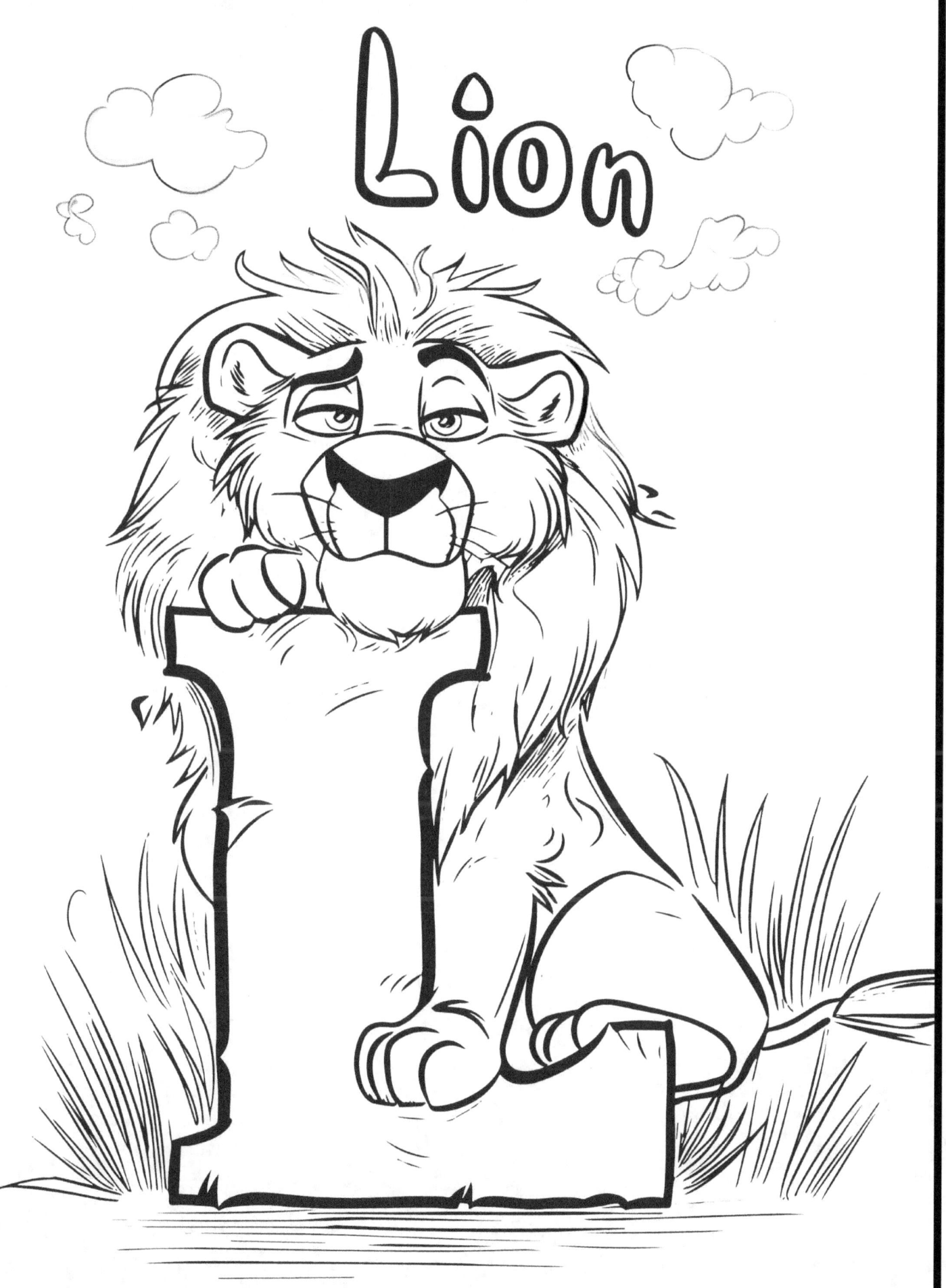

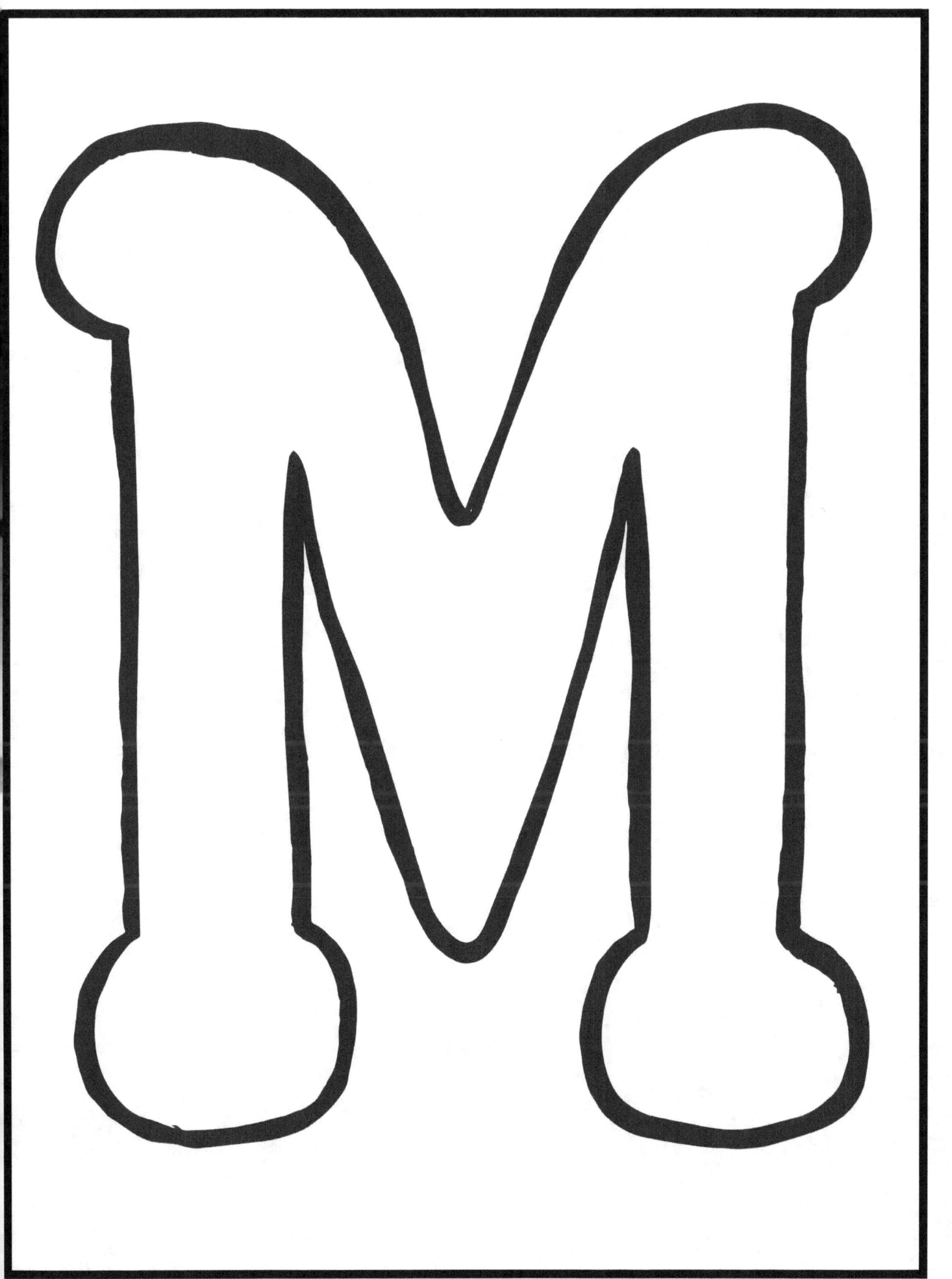

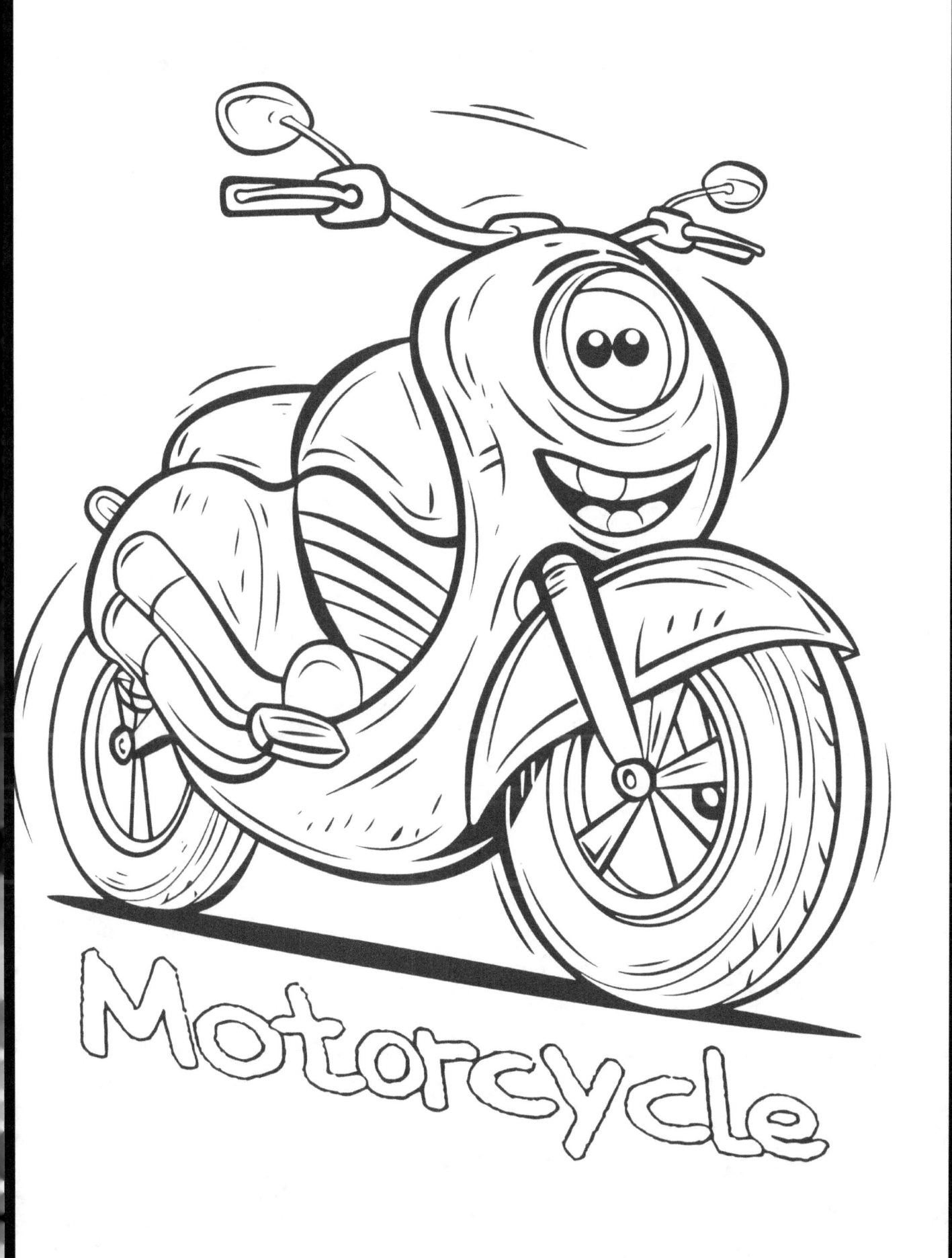

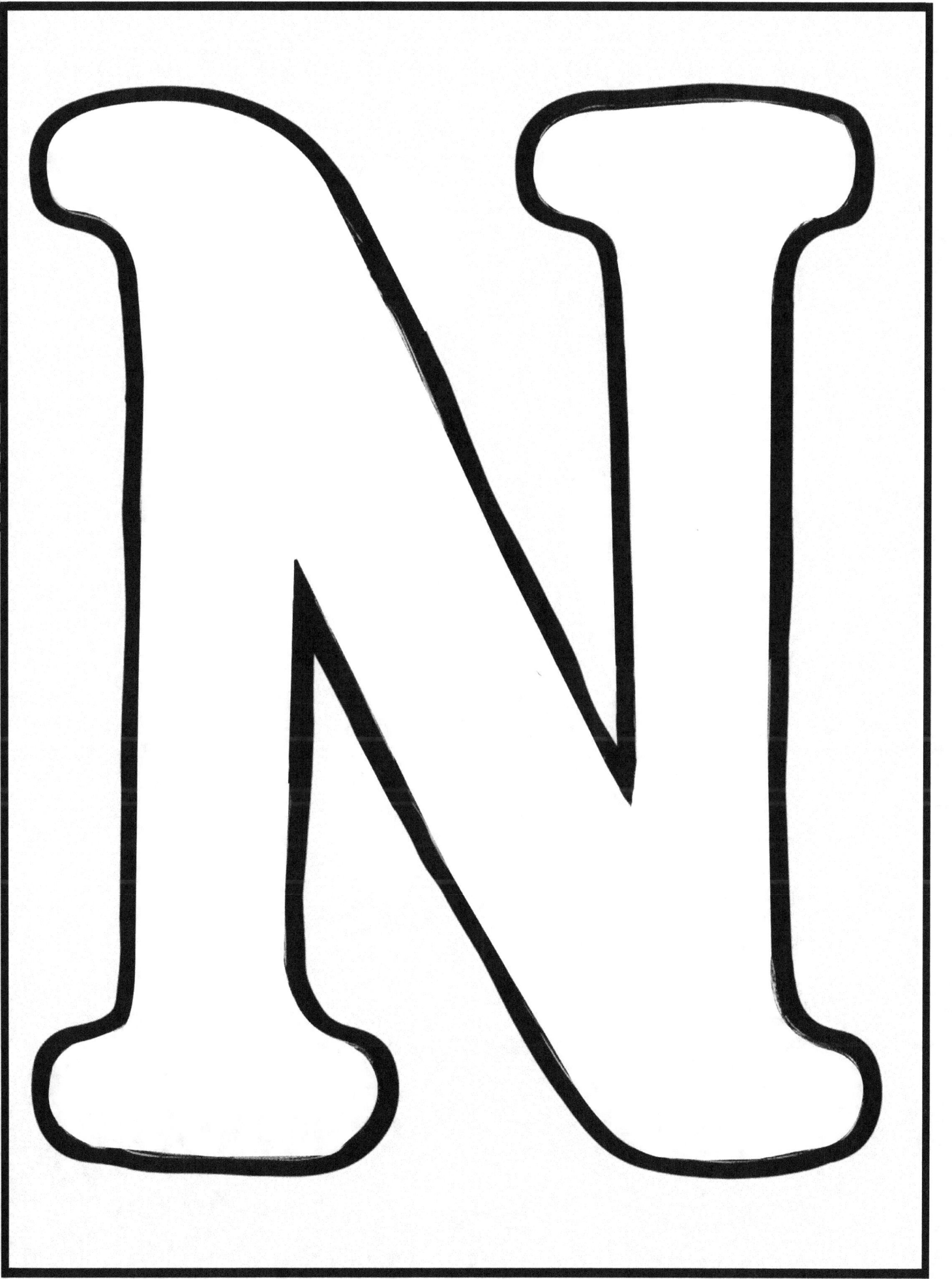

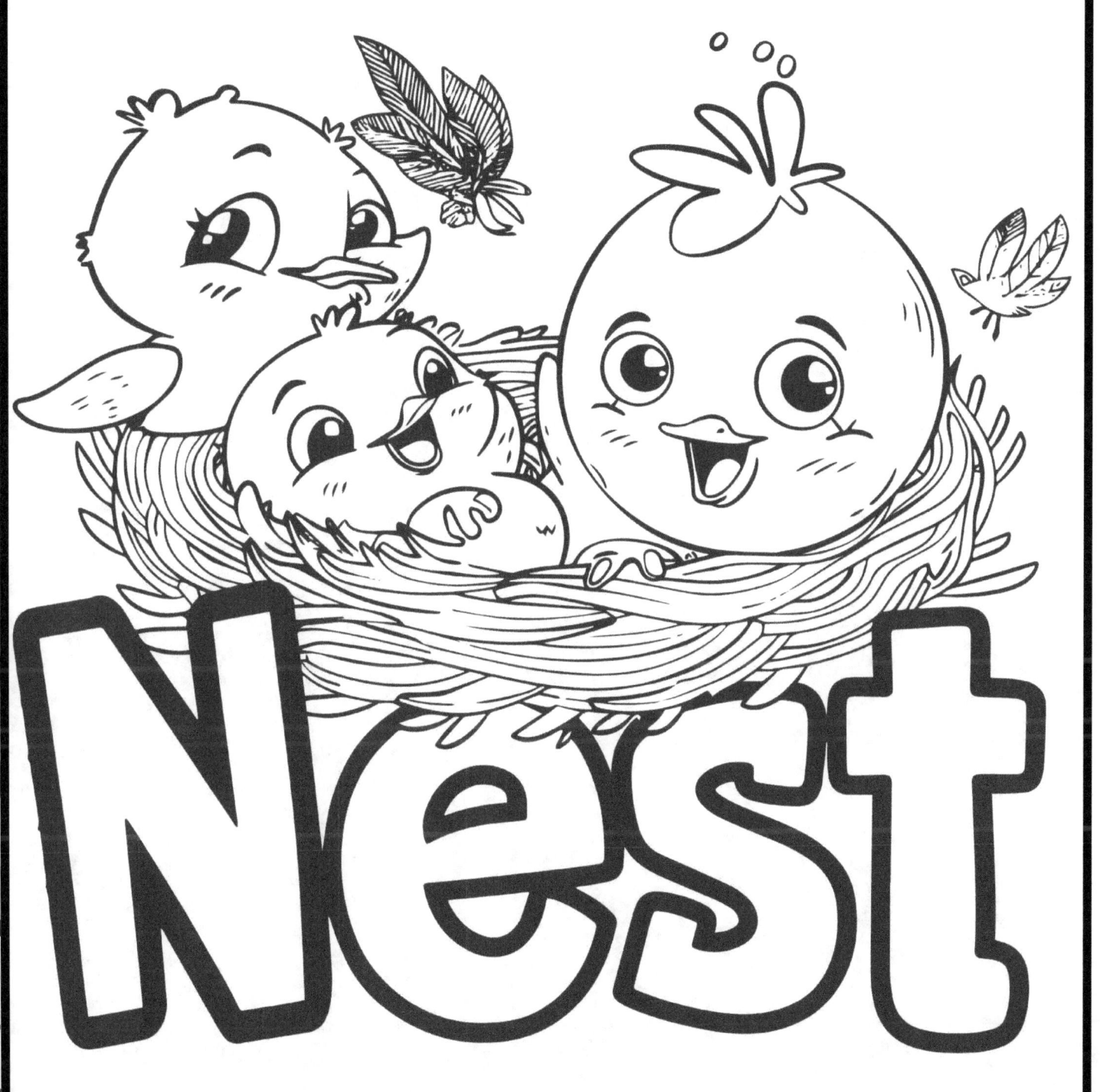

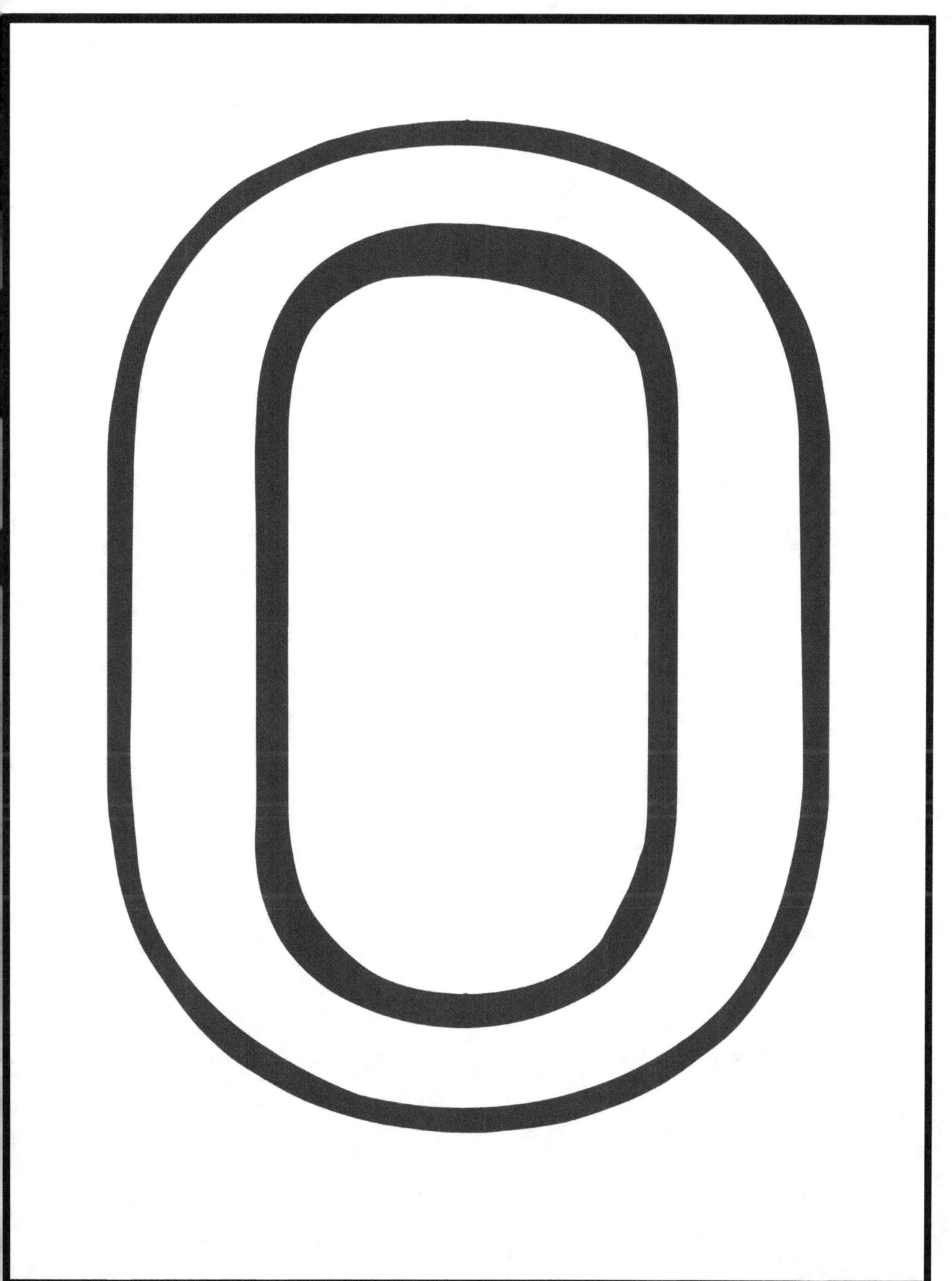

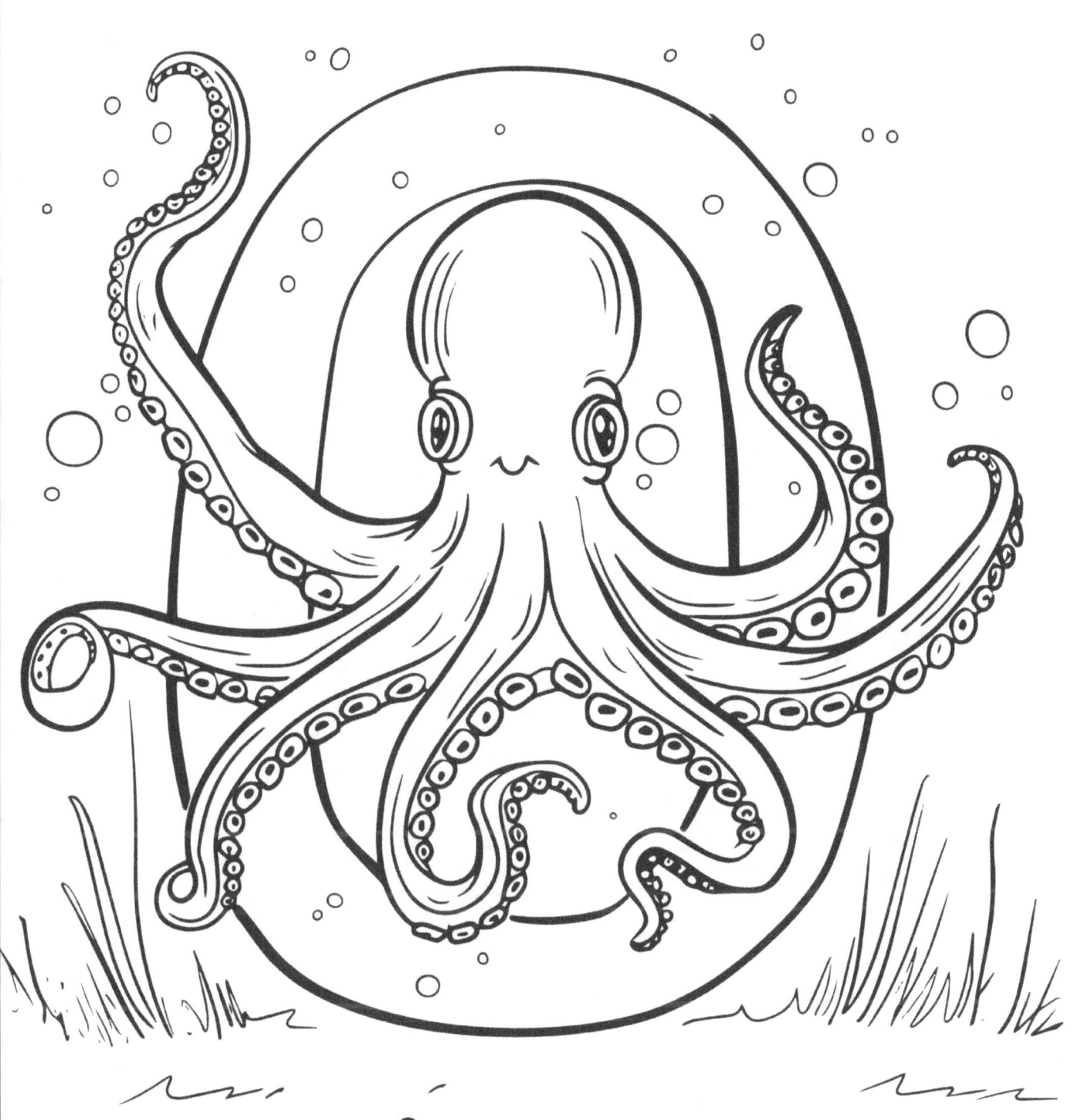

octopus

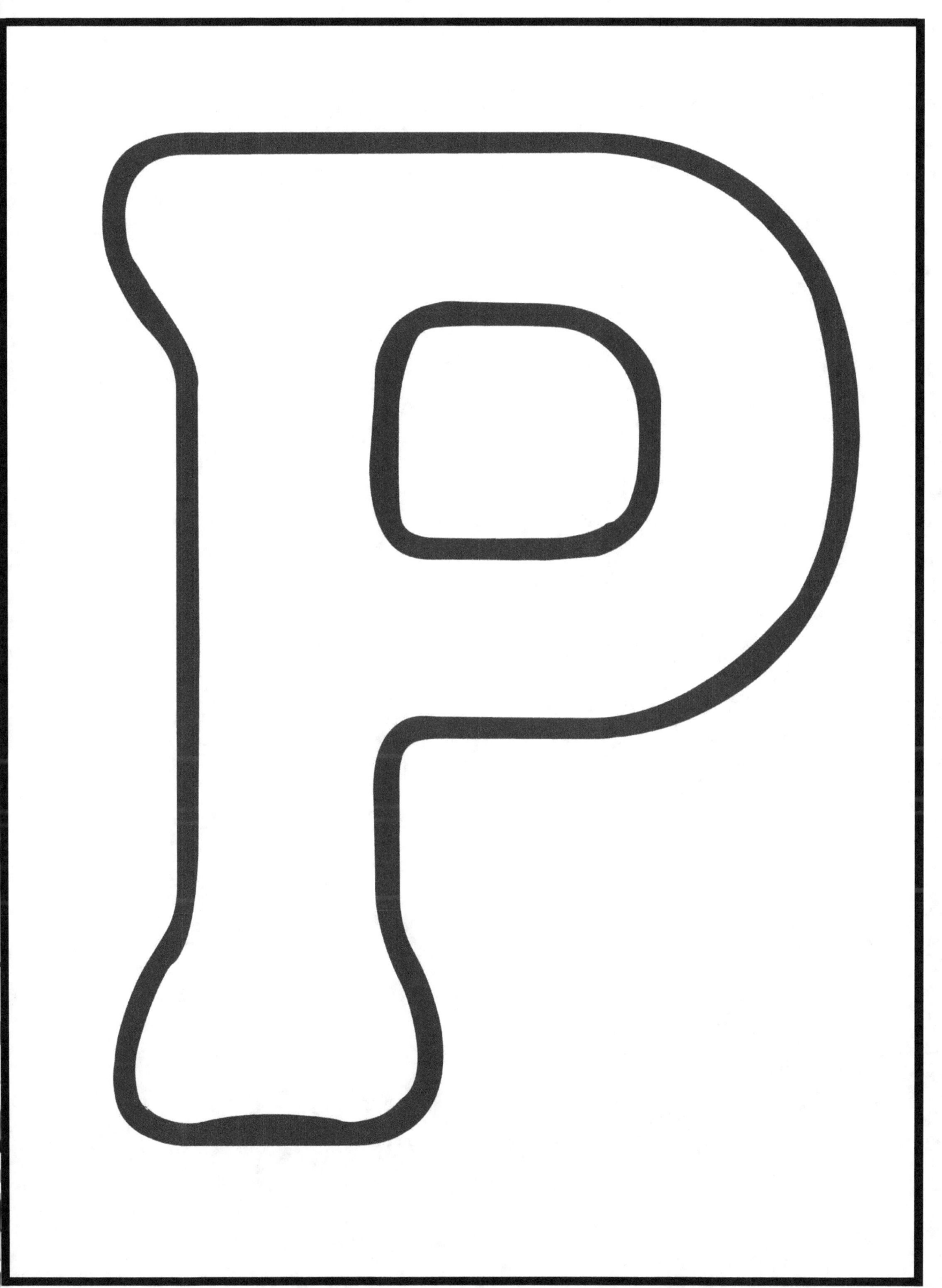

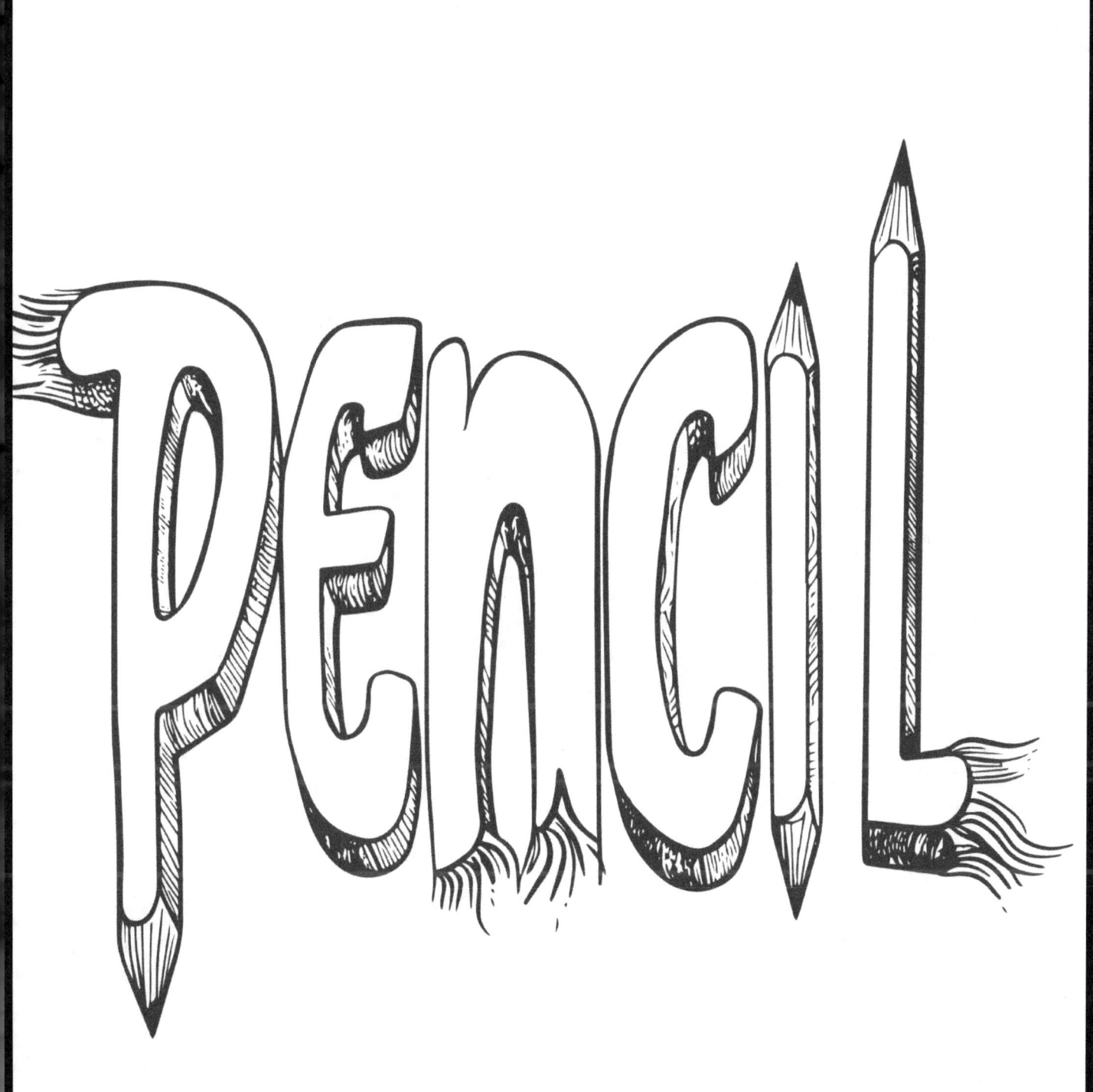

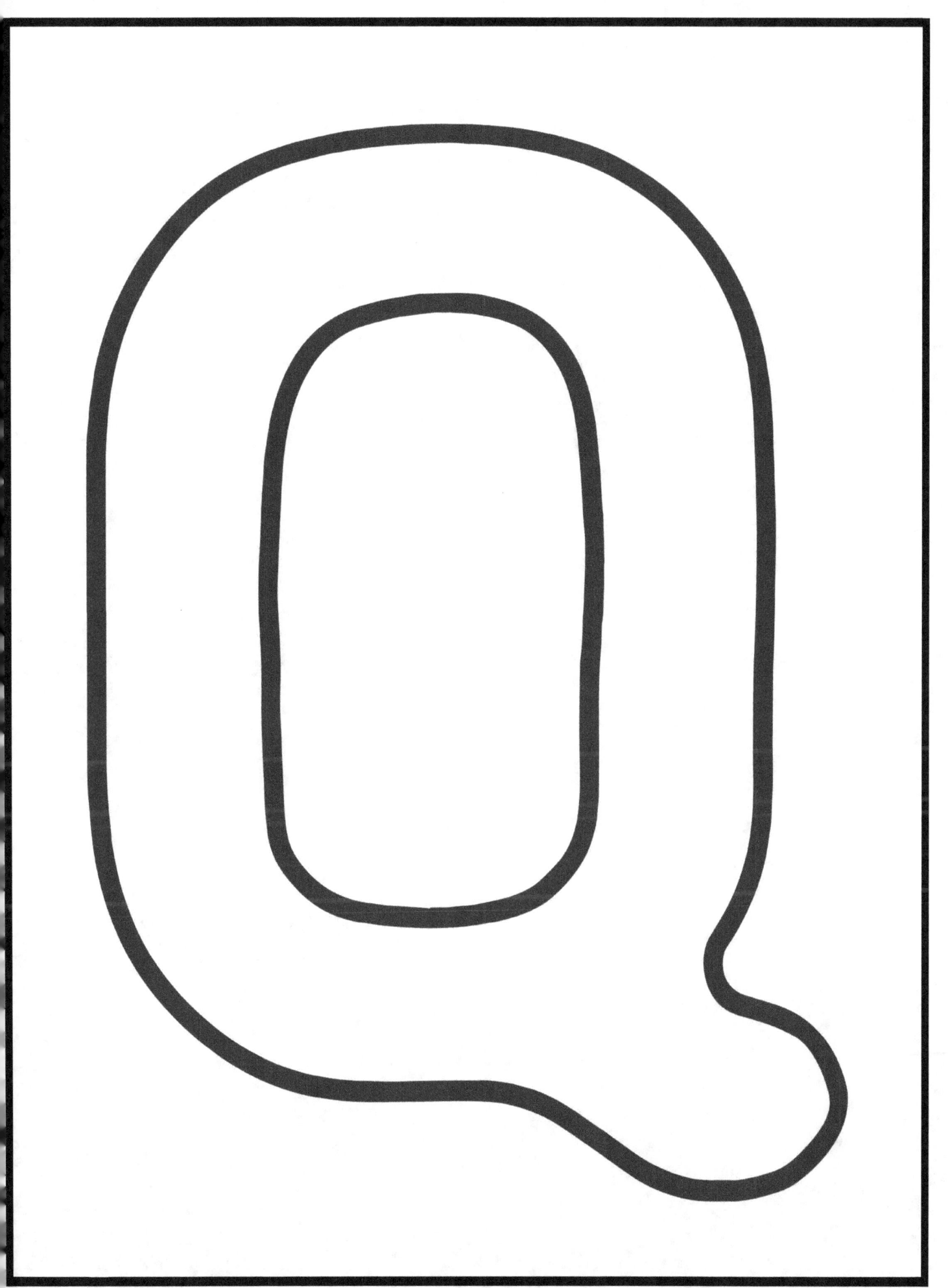

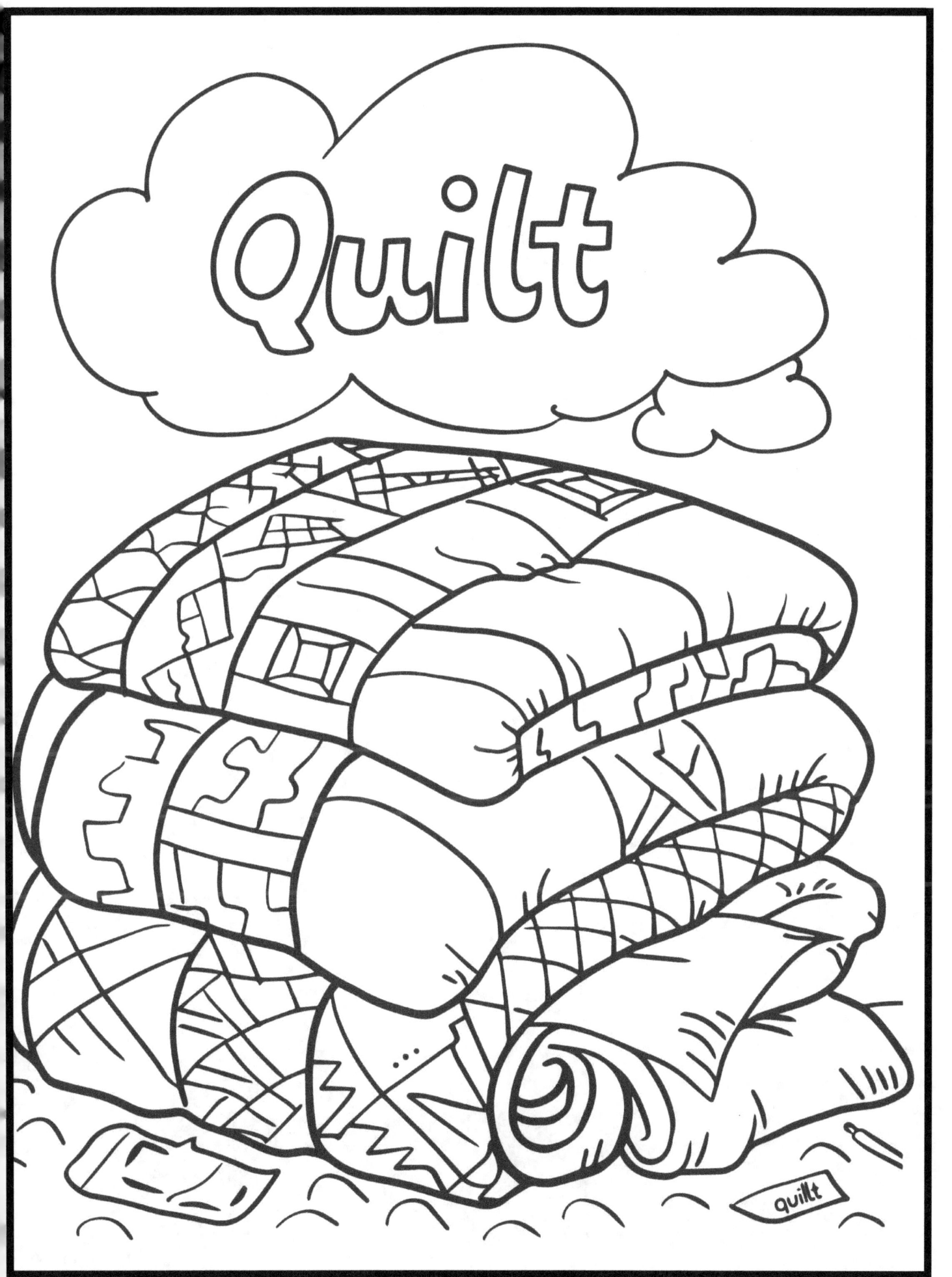

R

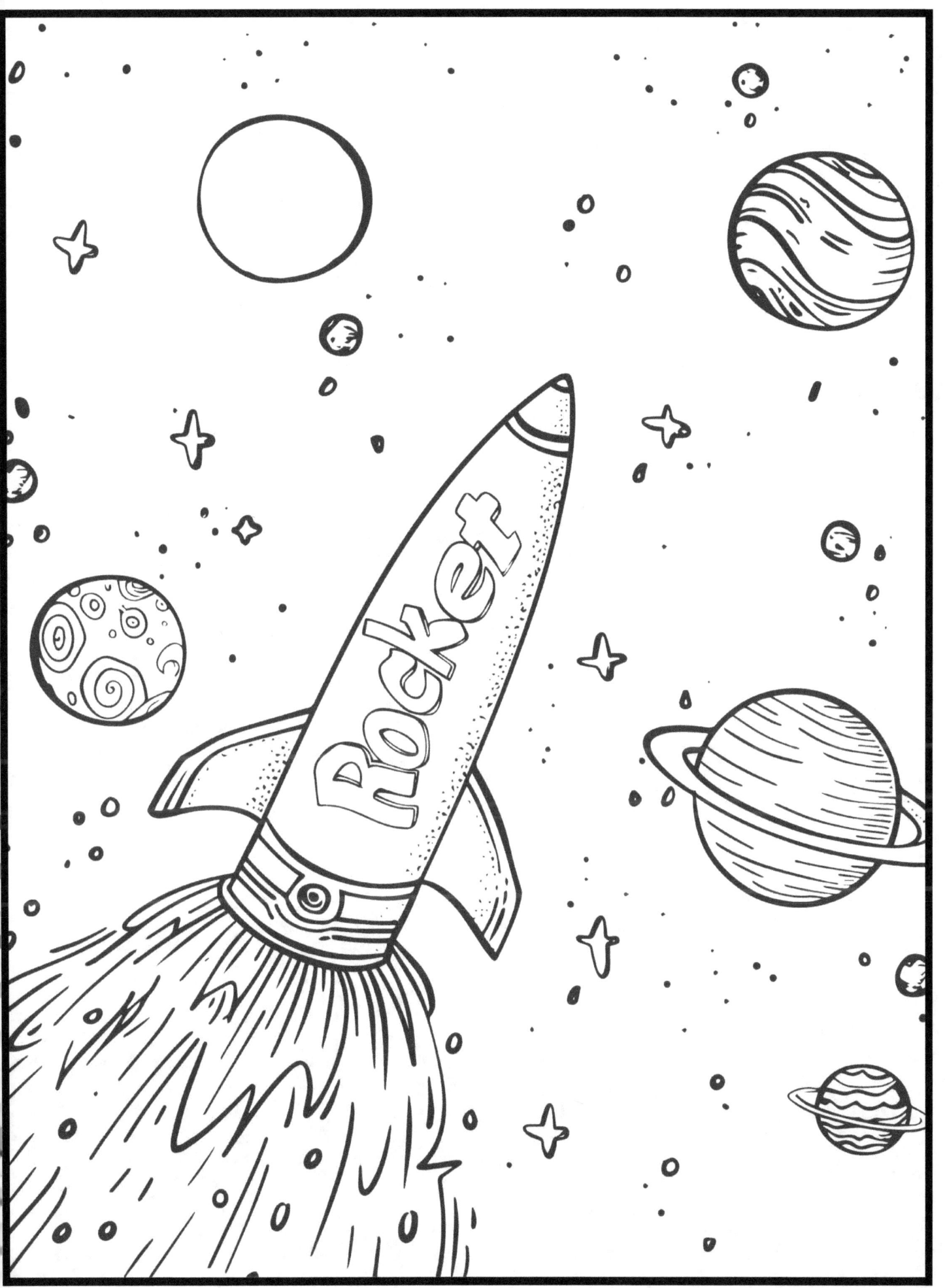

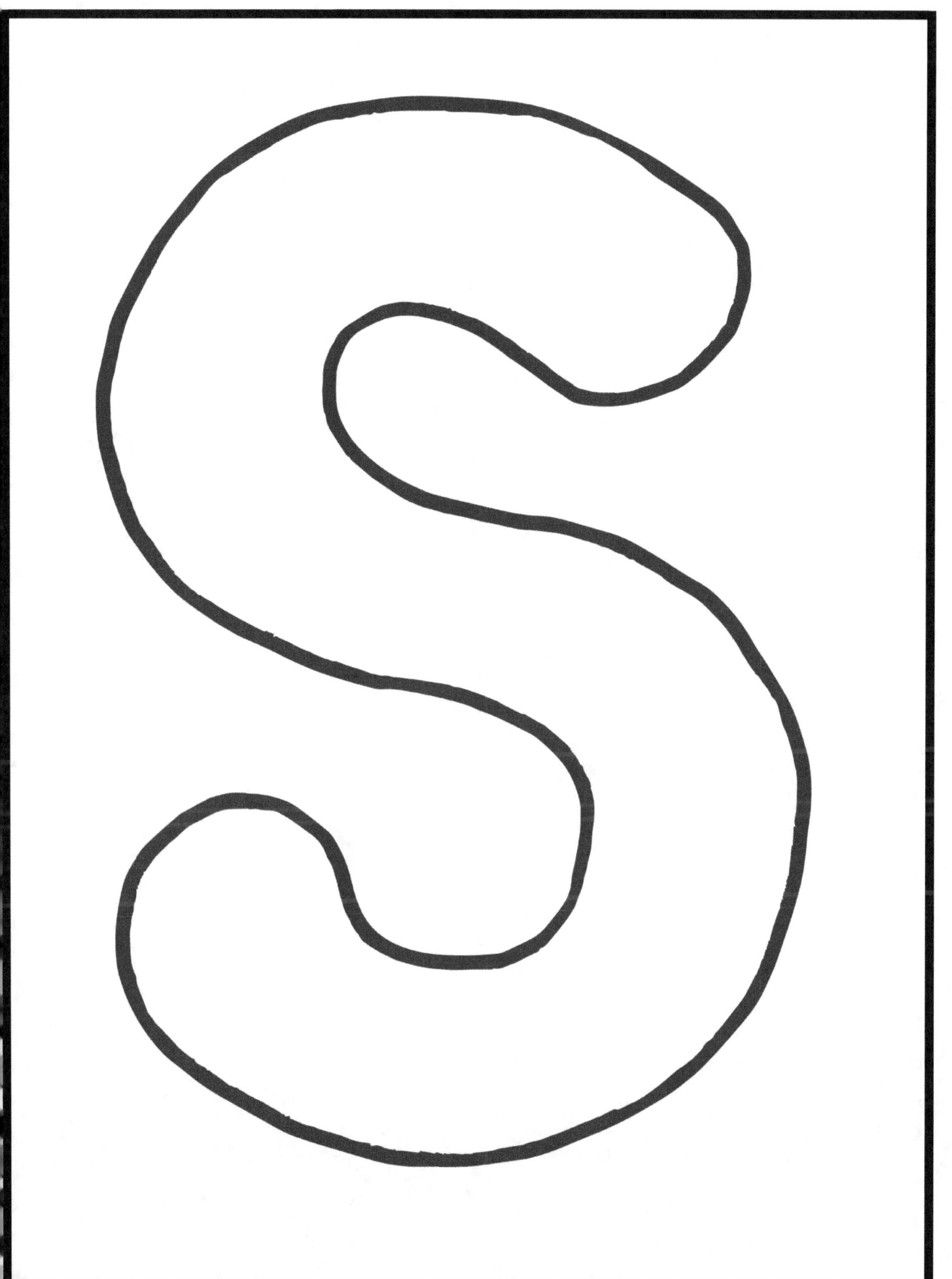

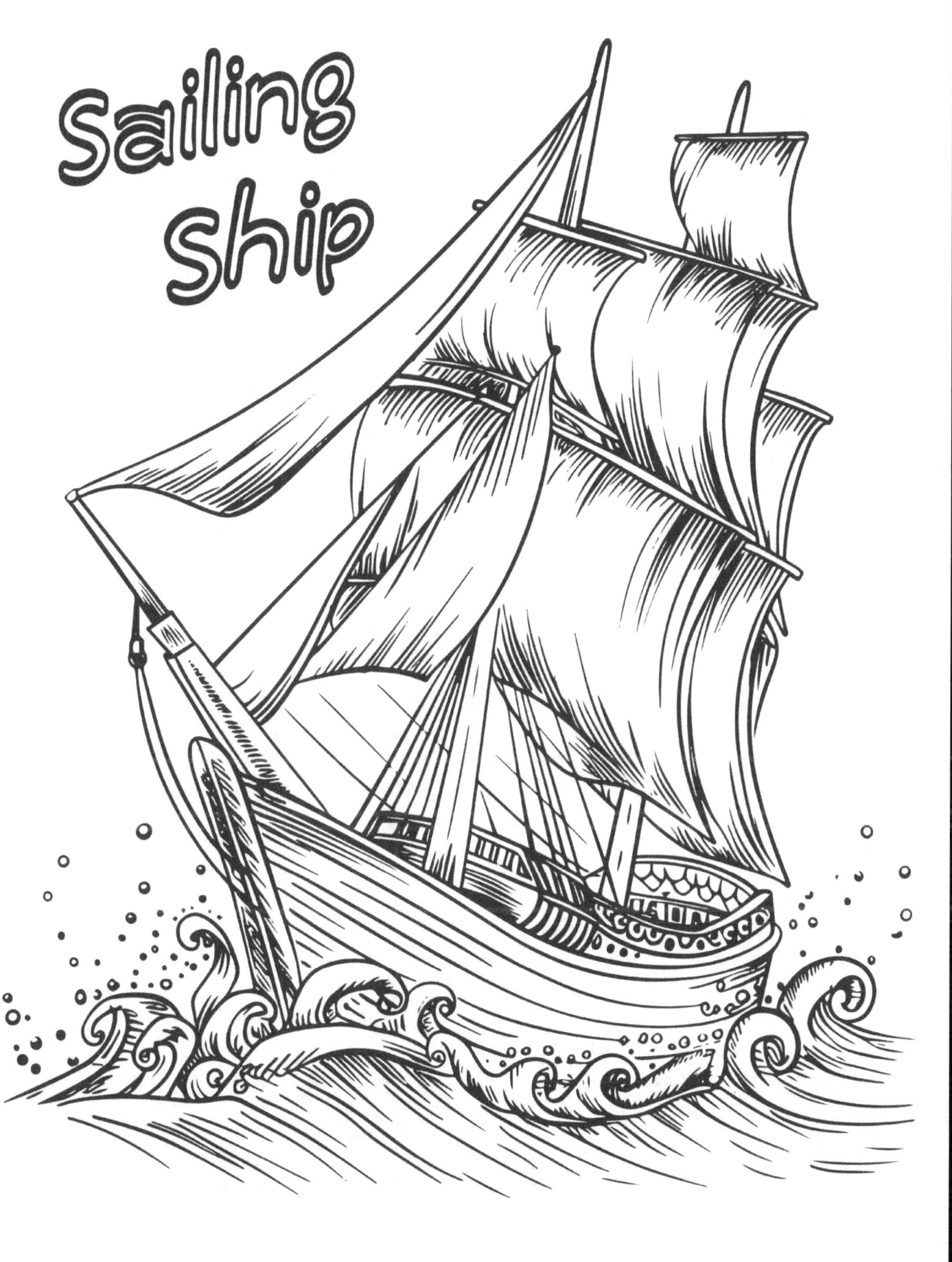

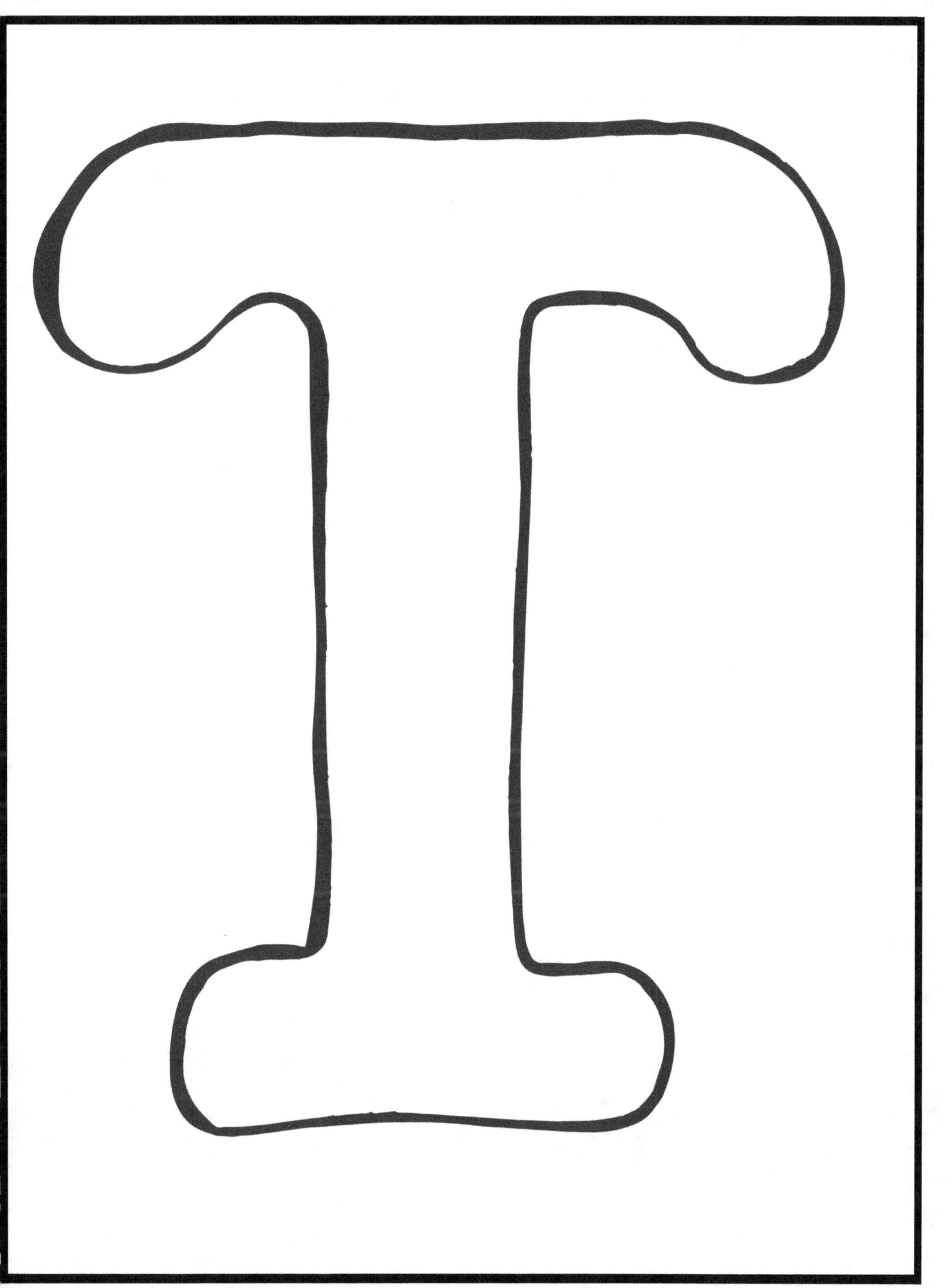

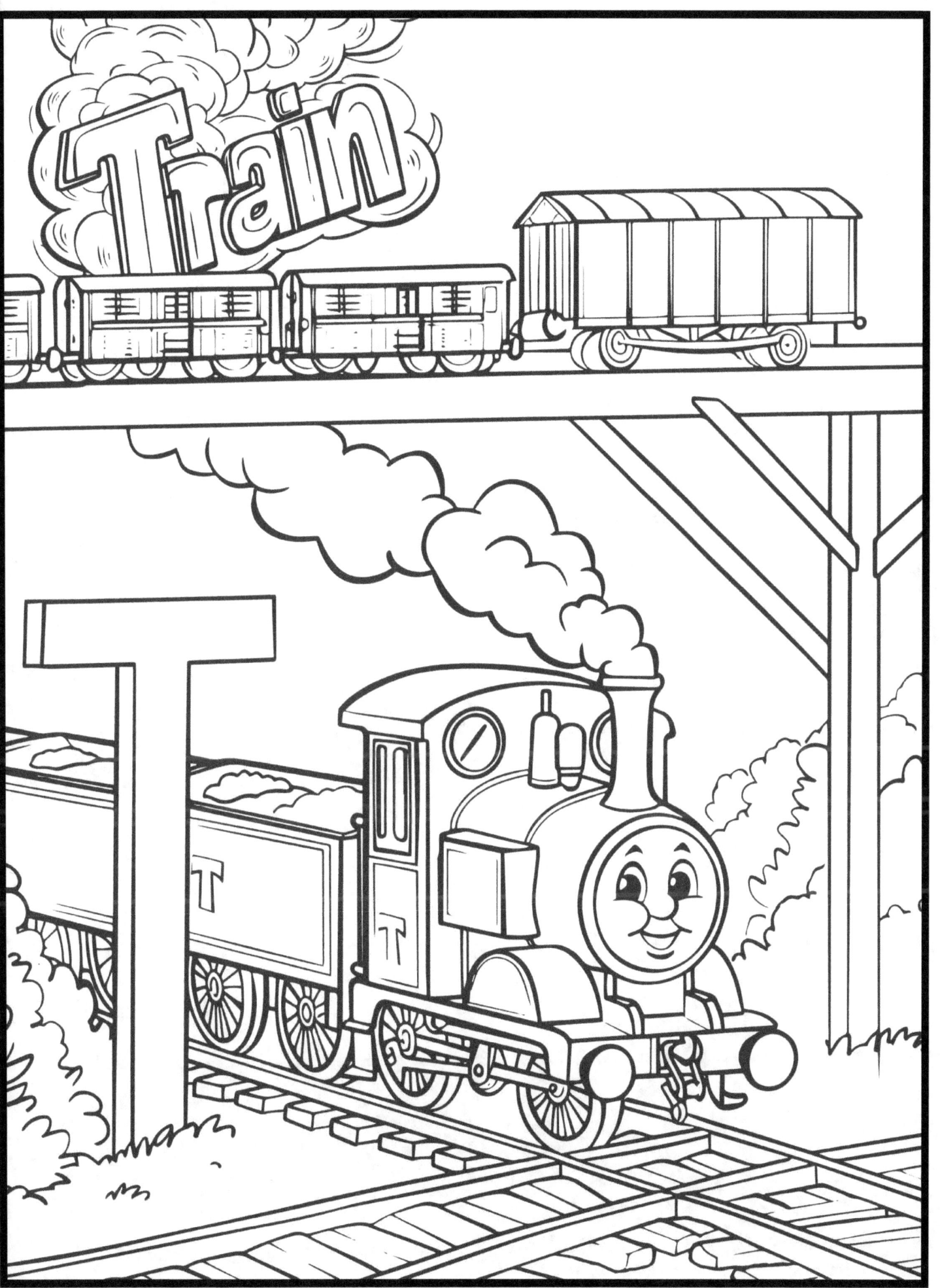

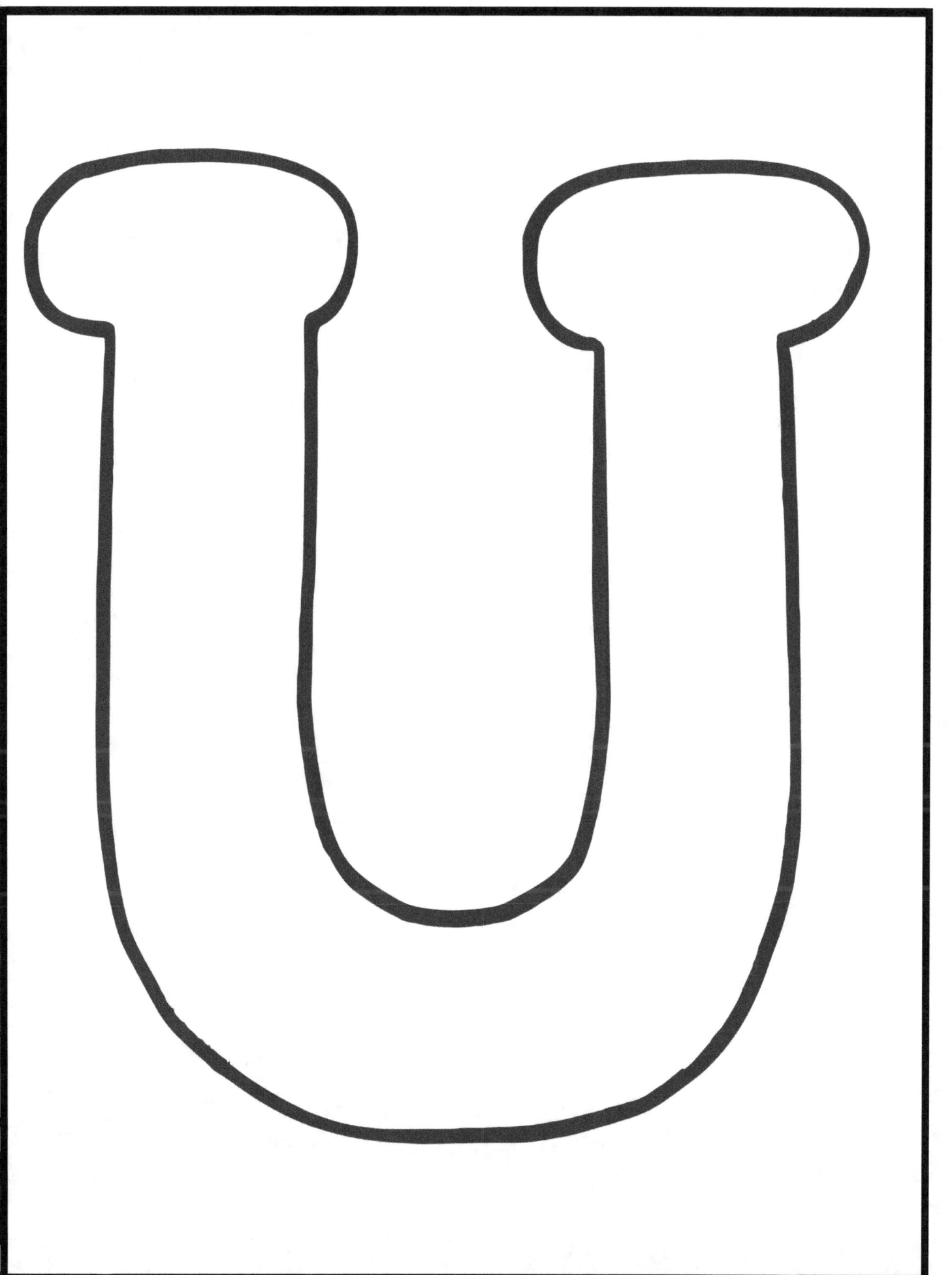

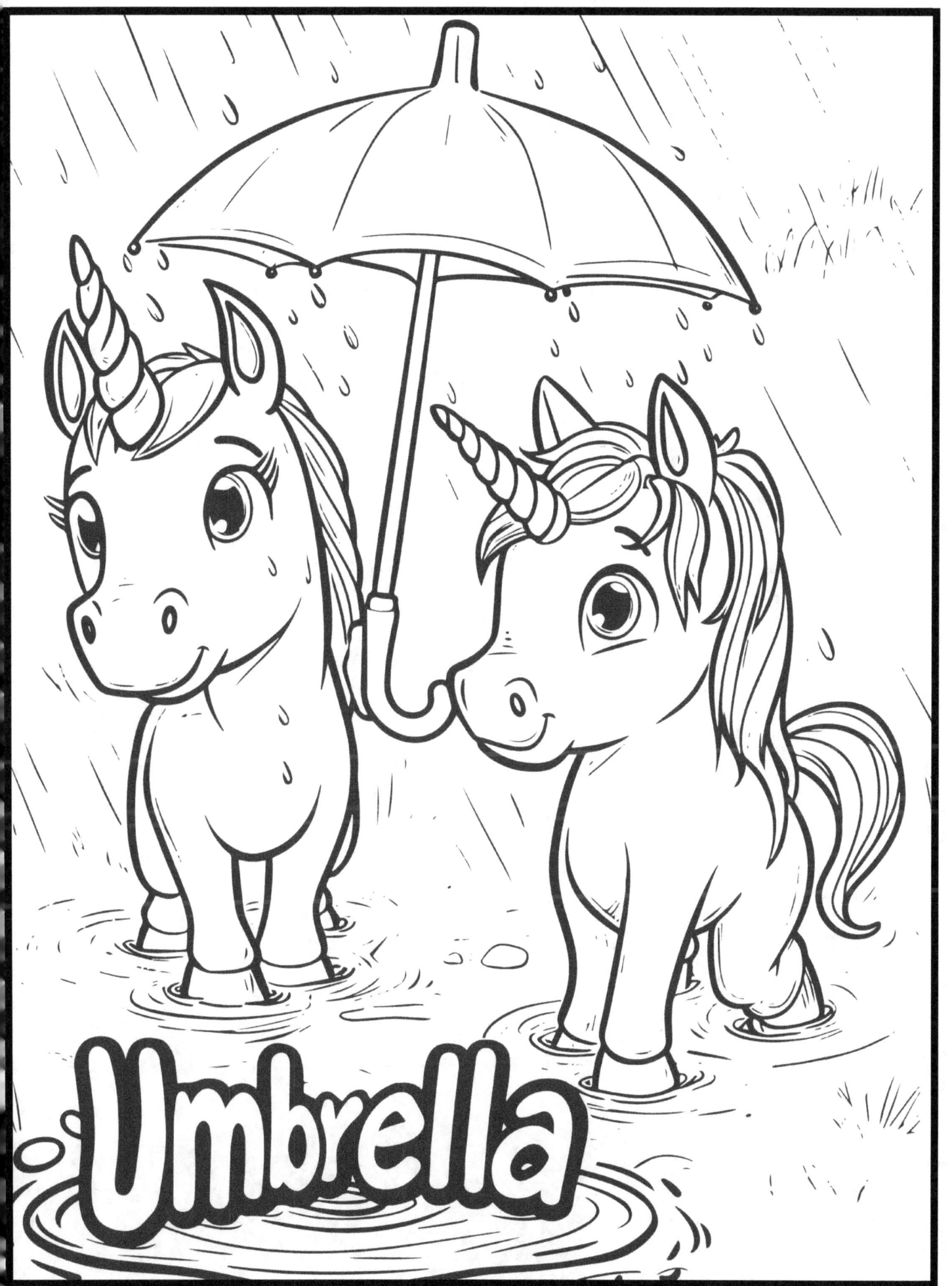

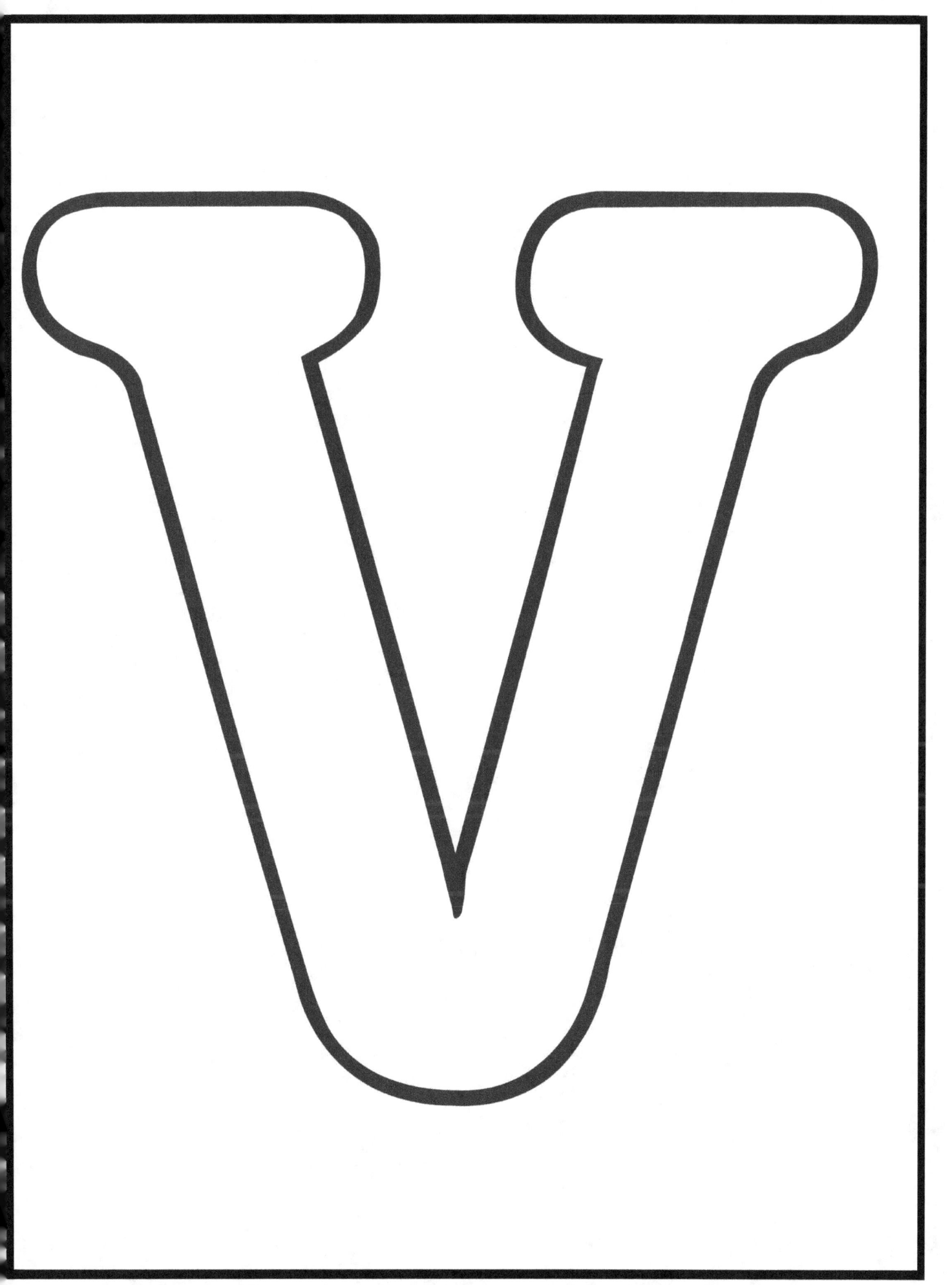

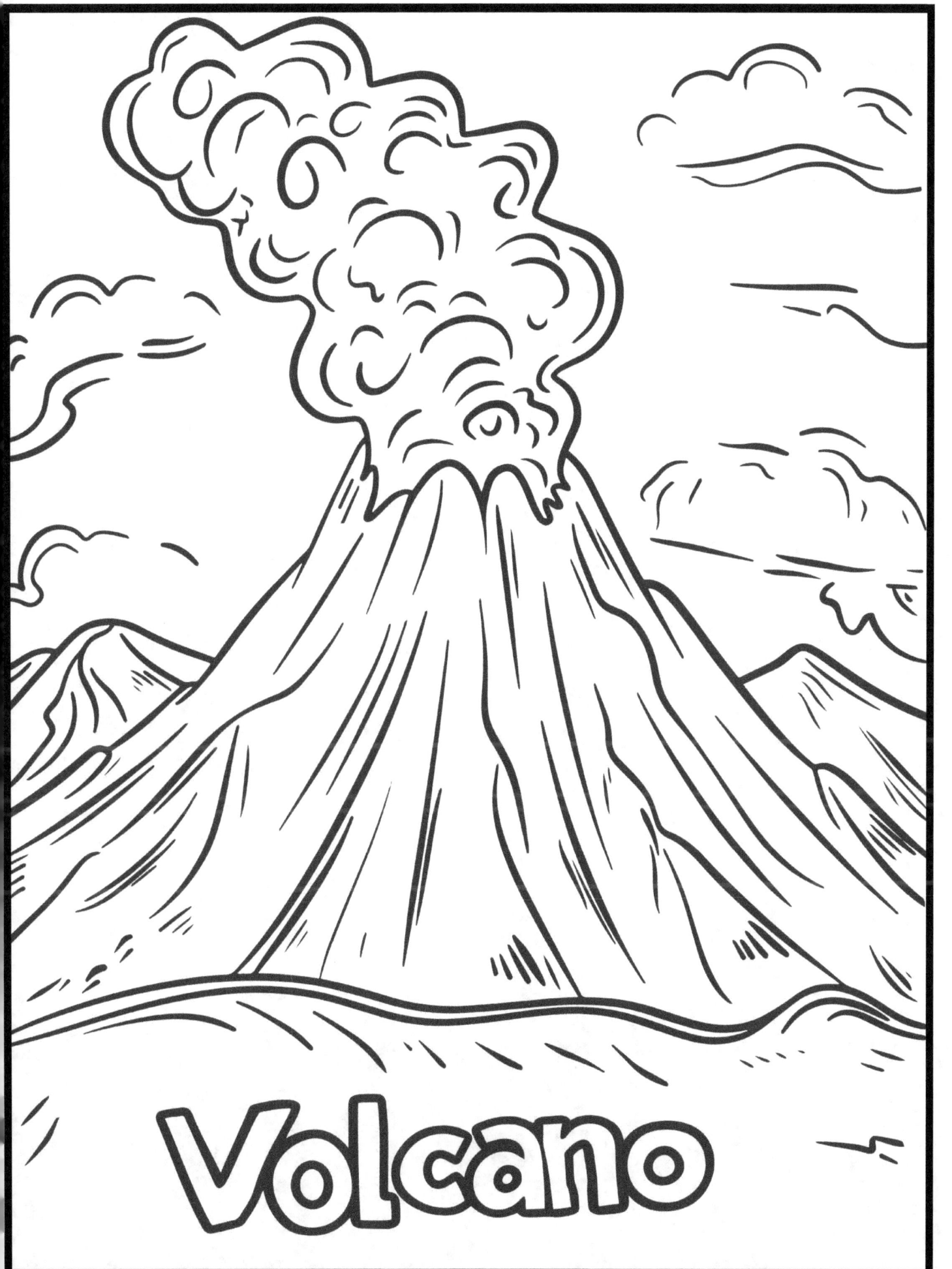

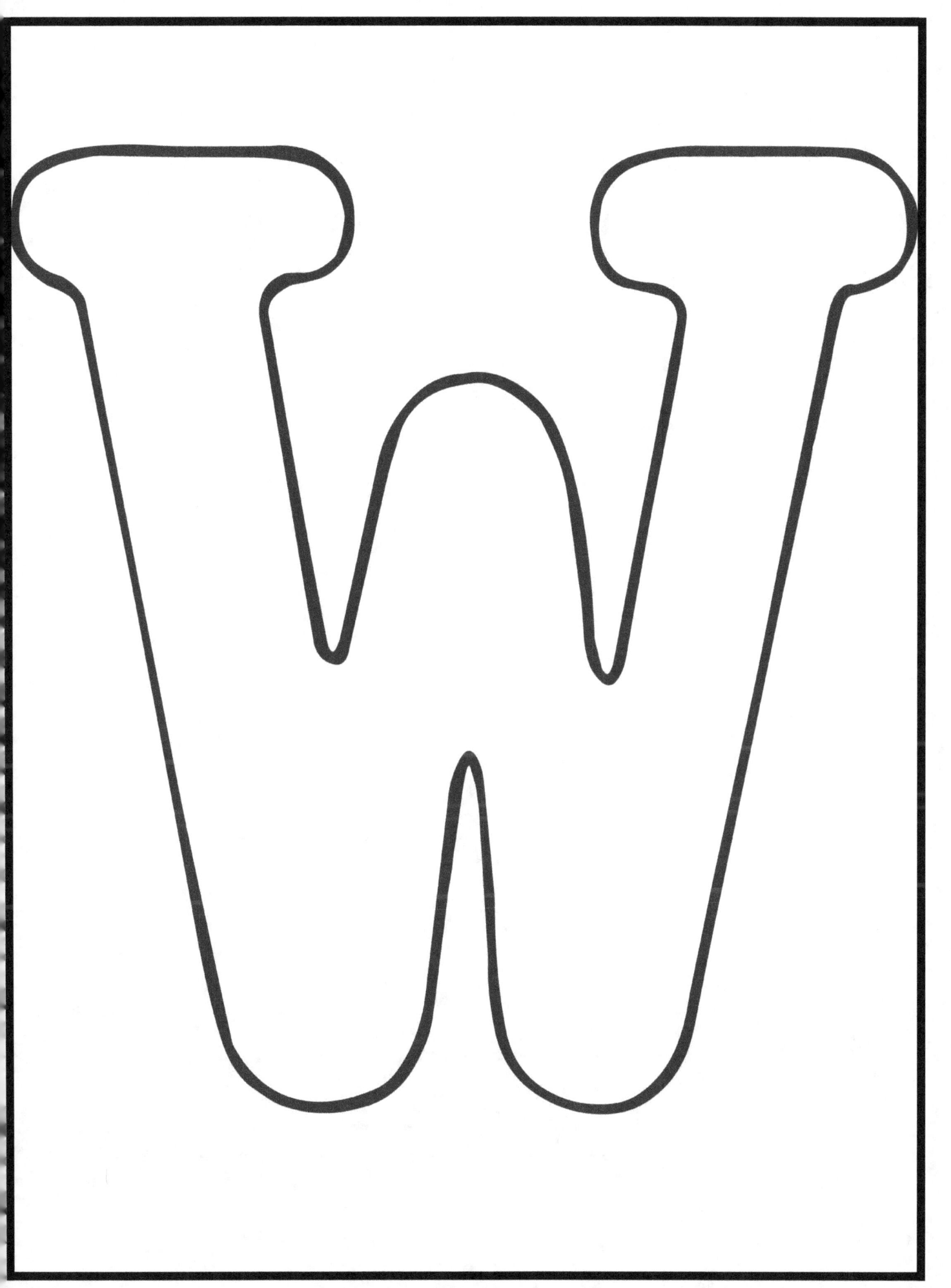

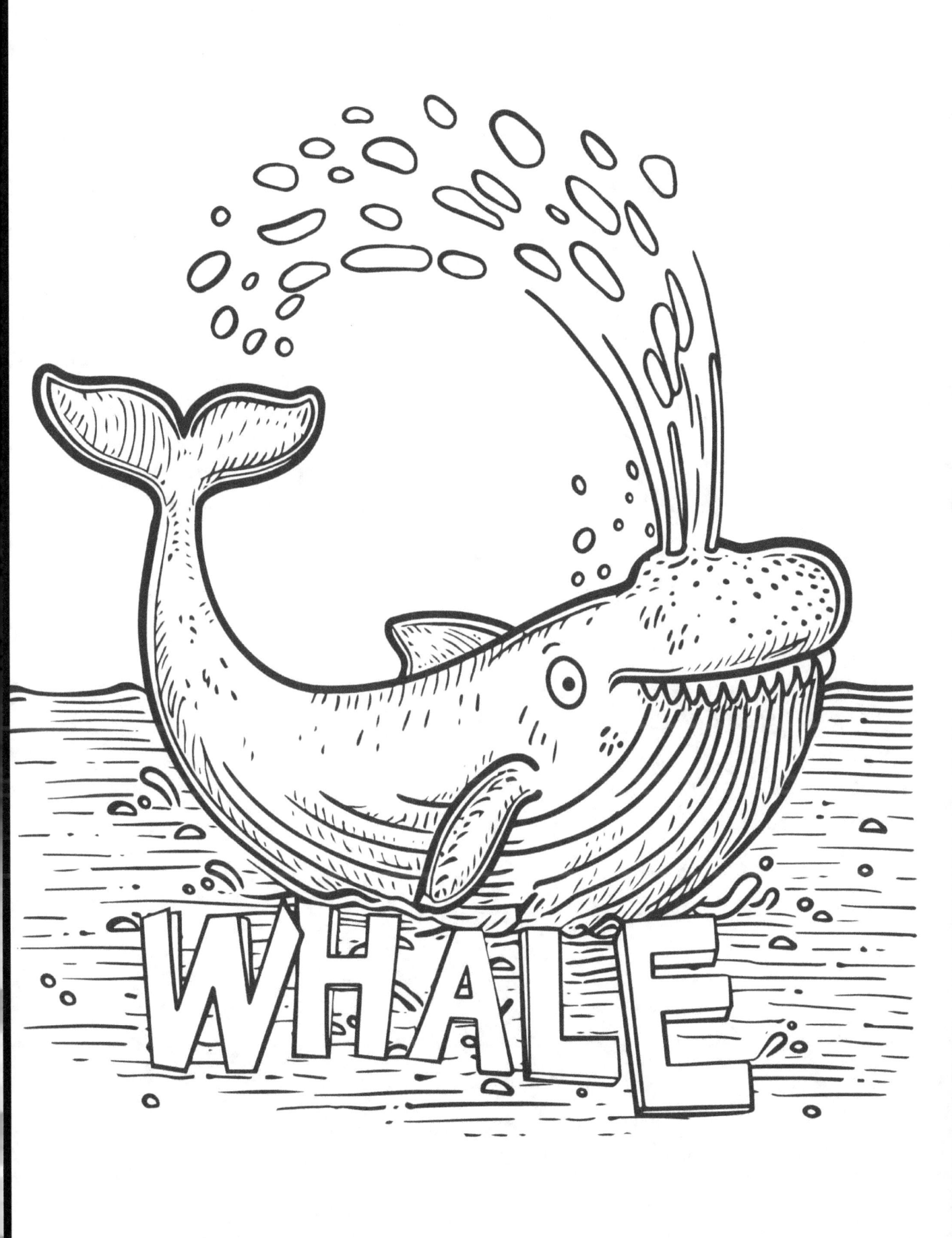

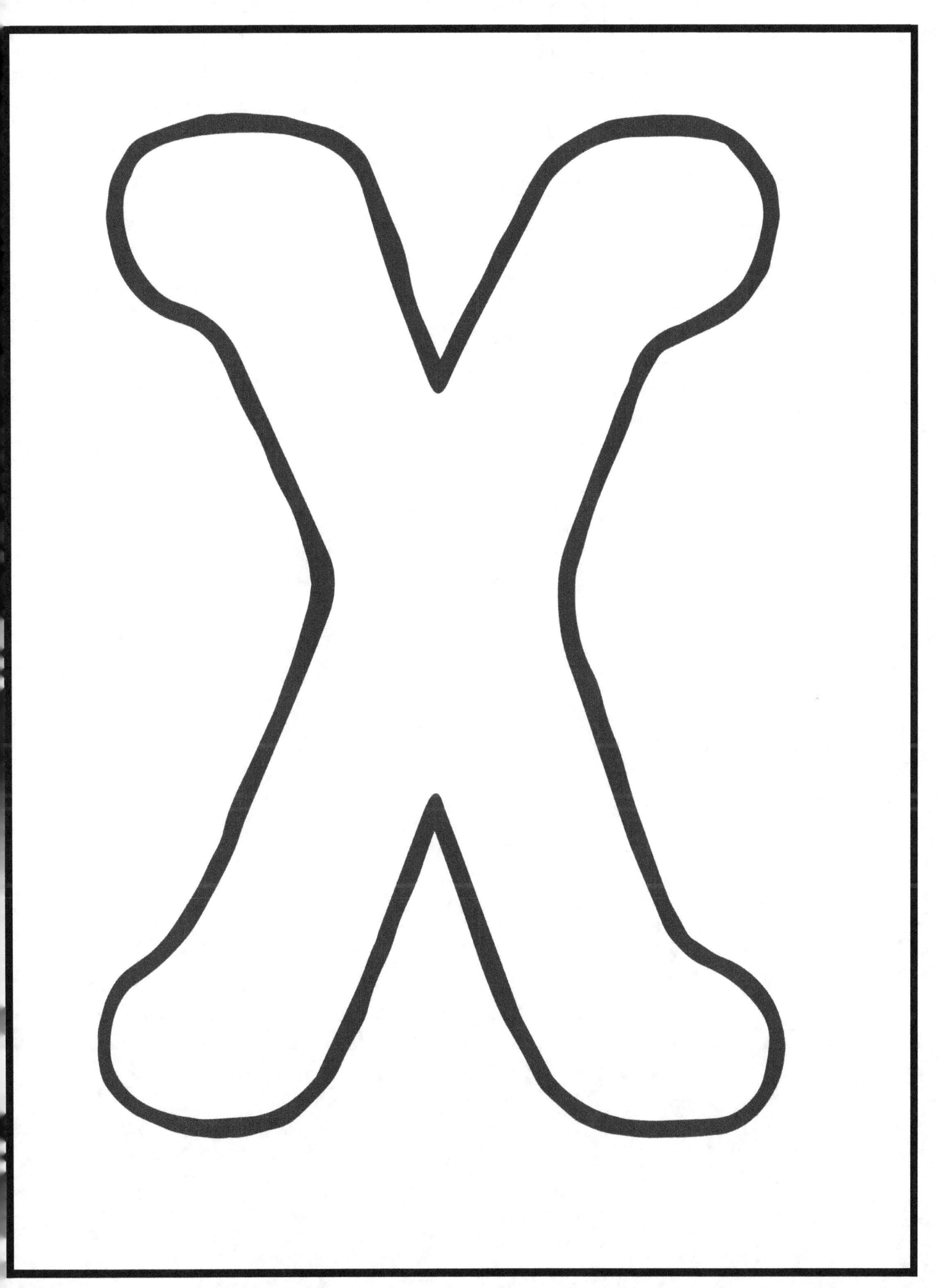

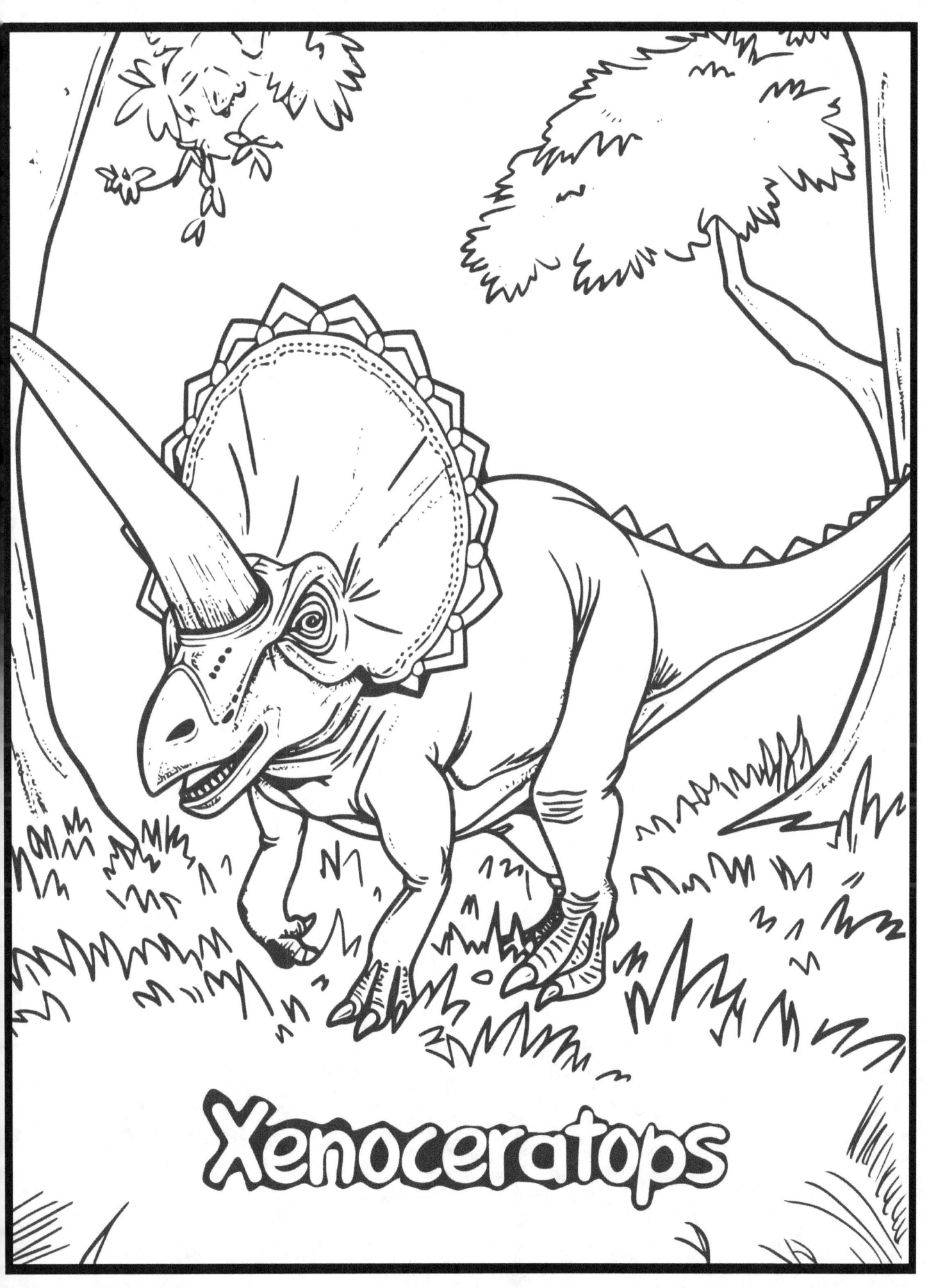

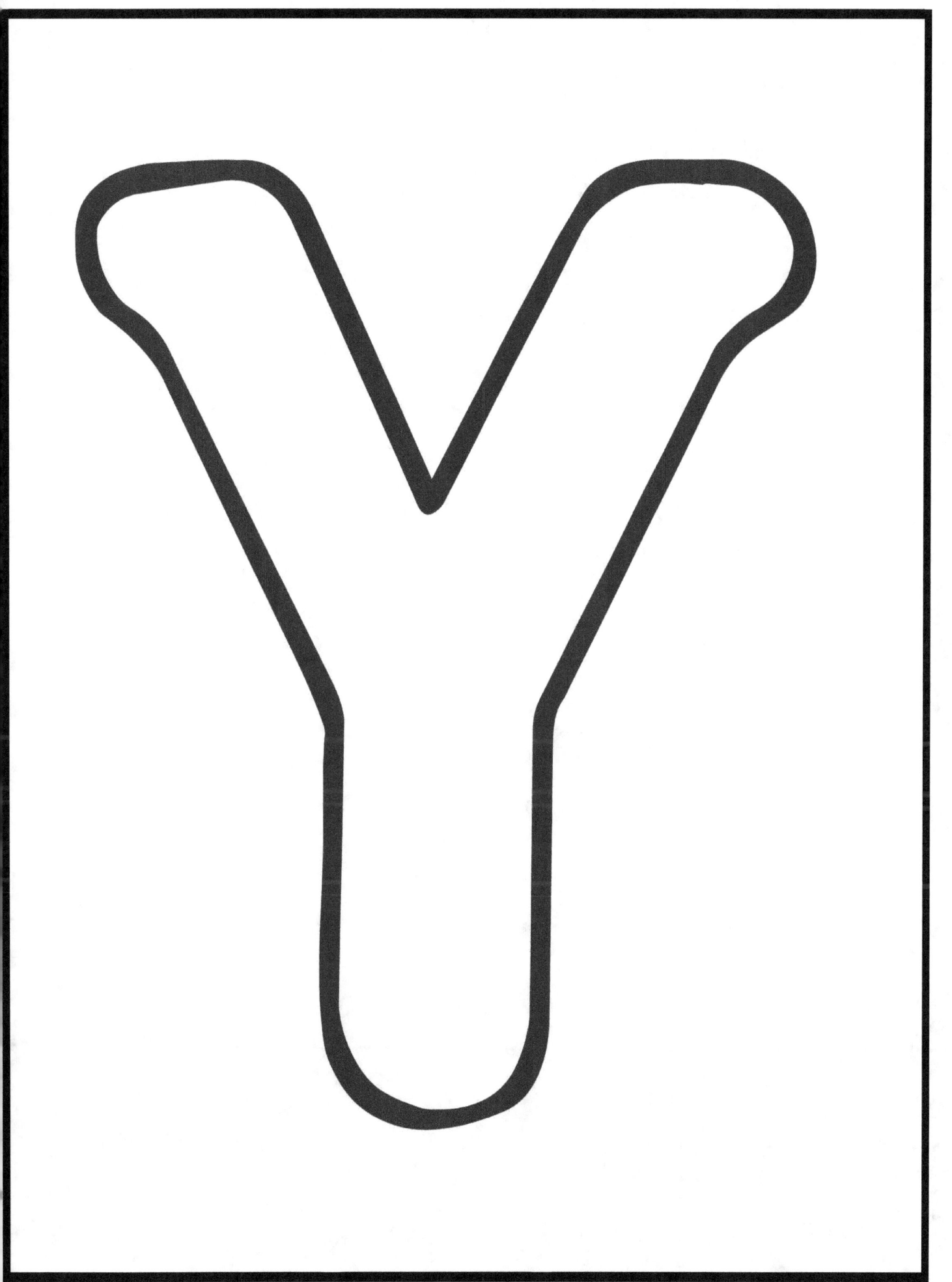

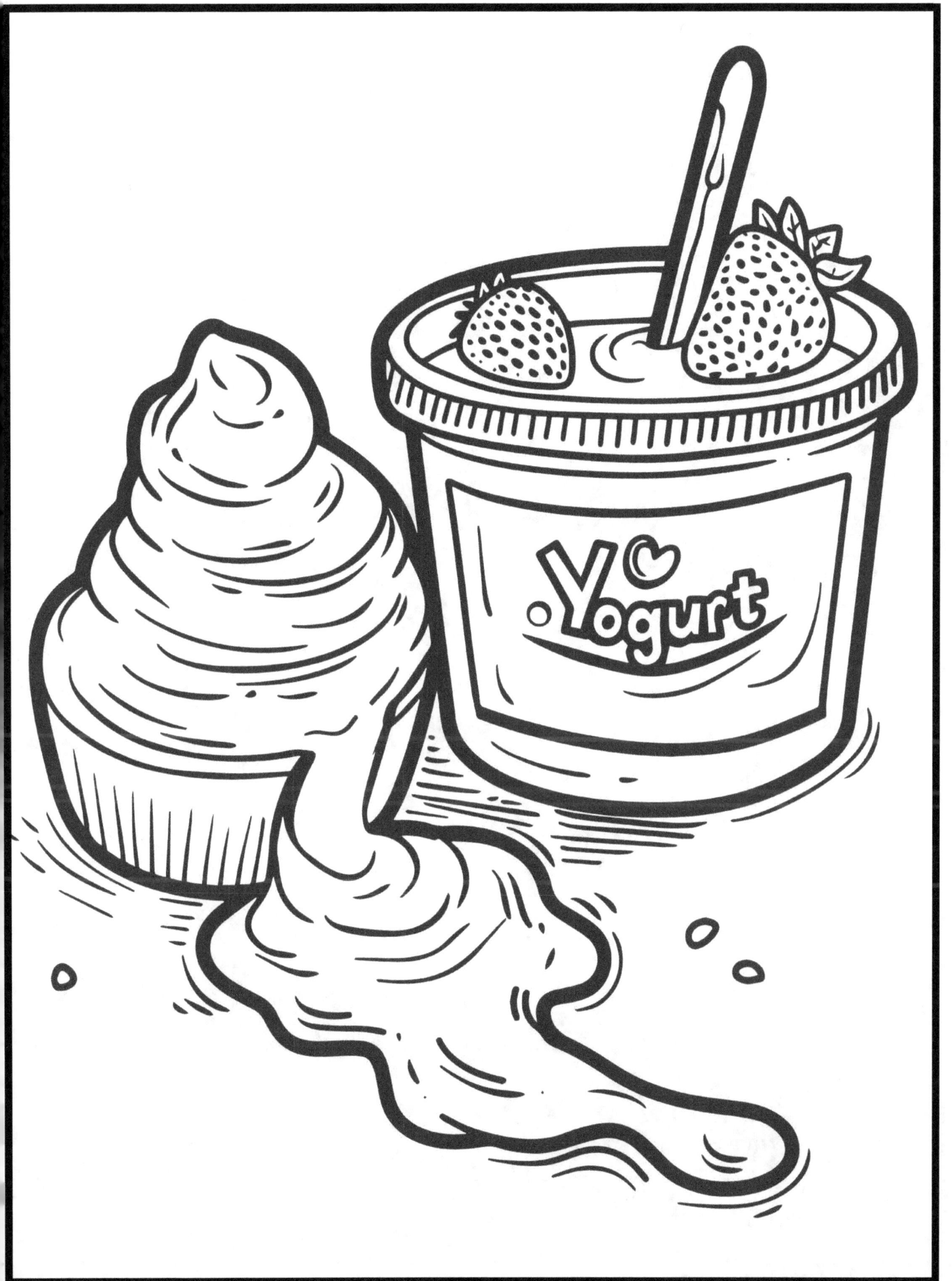

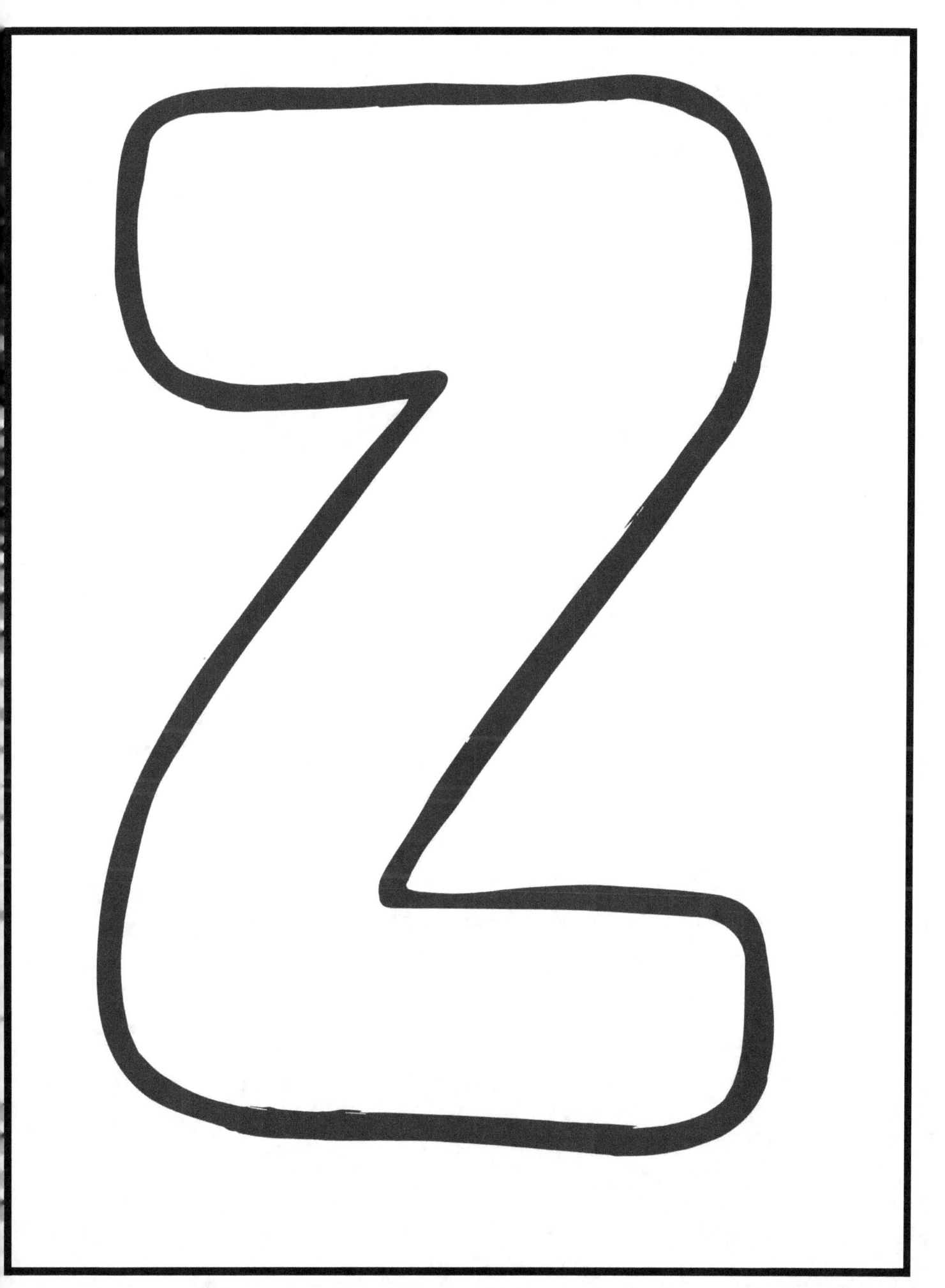

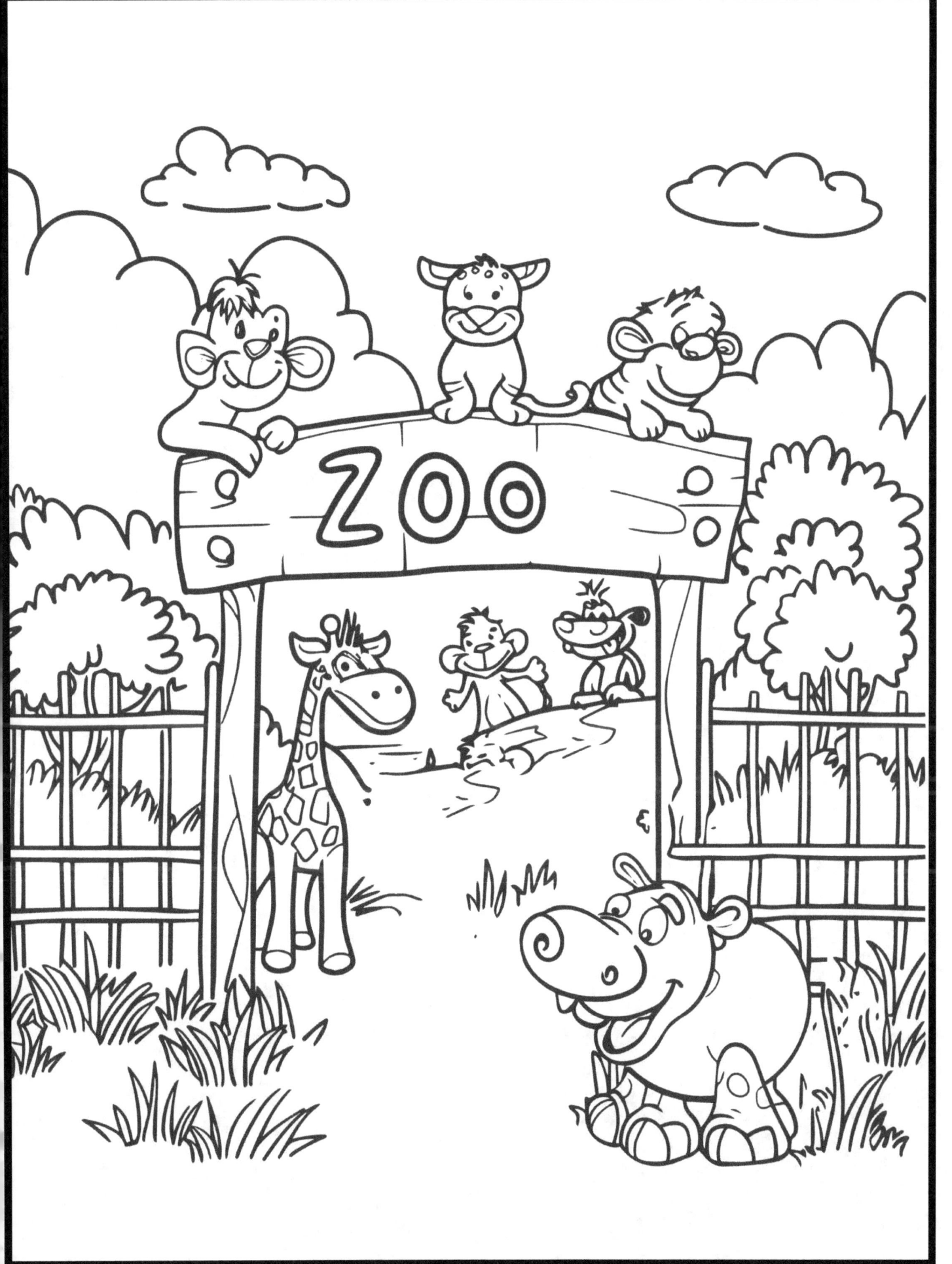

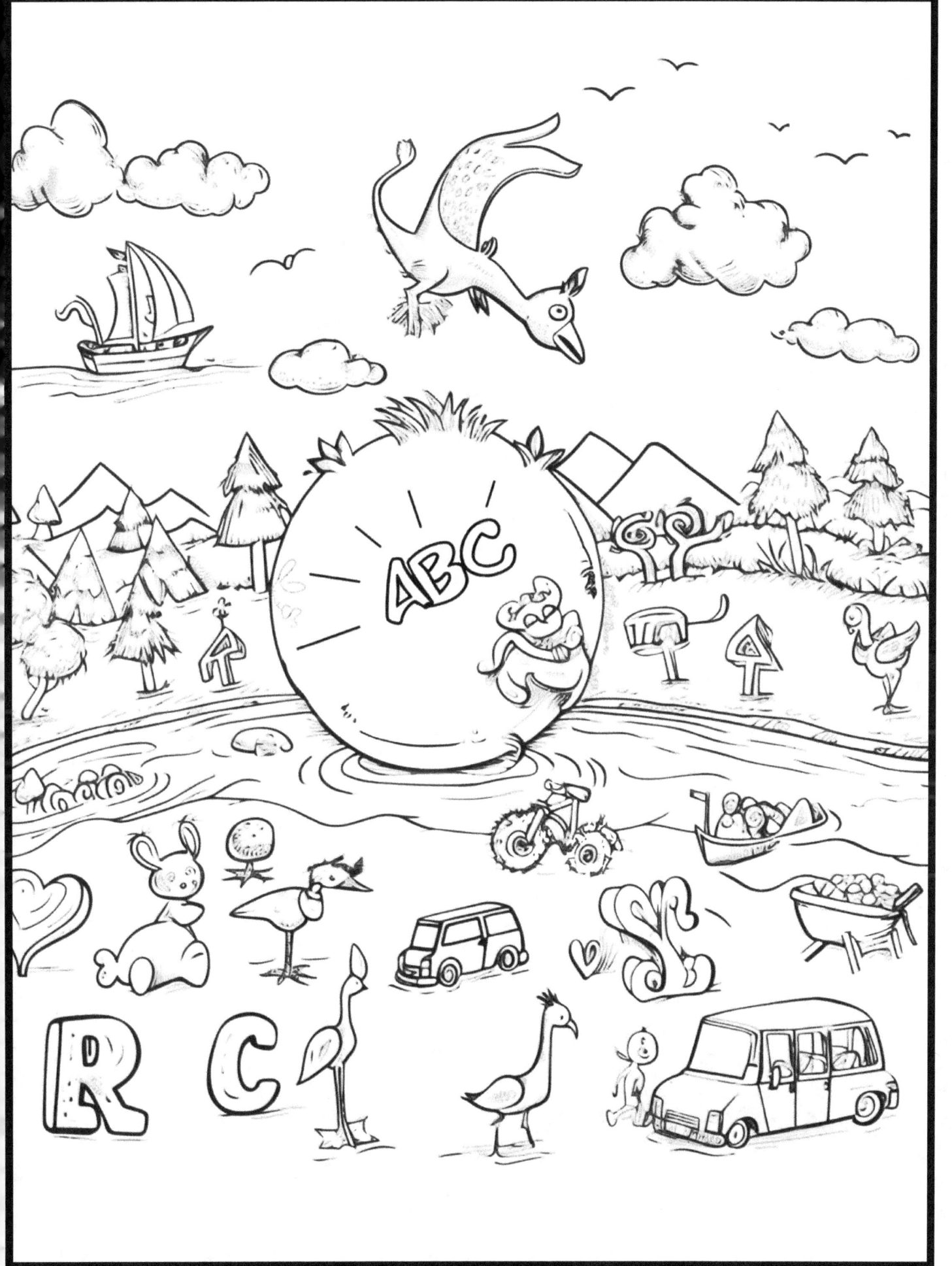

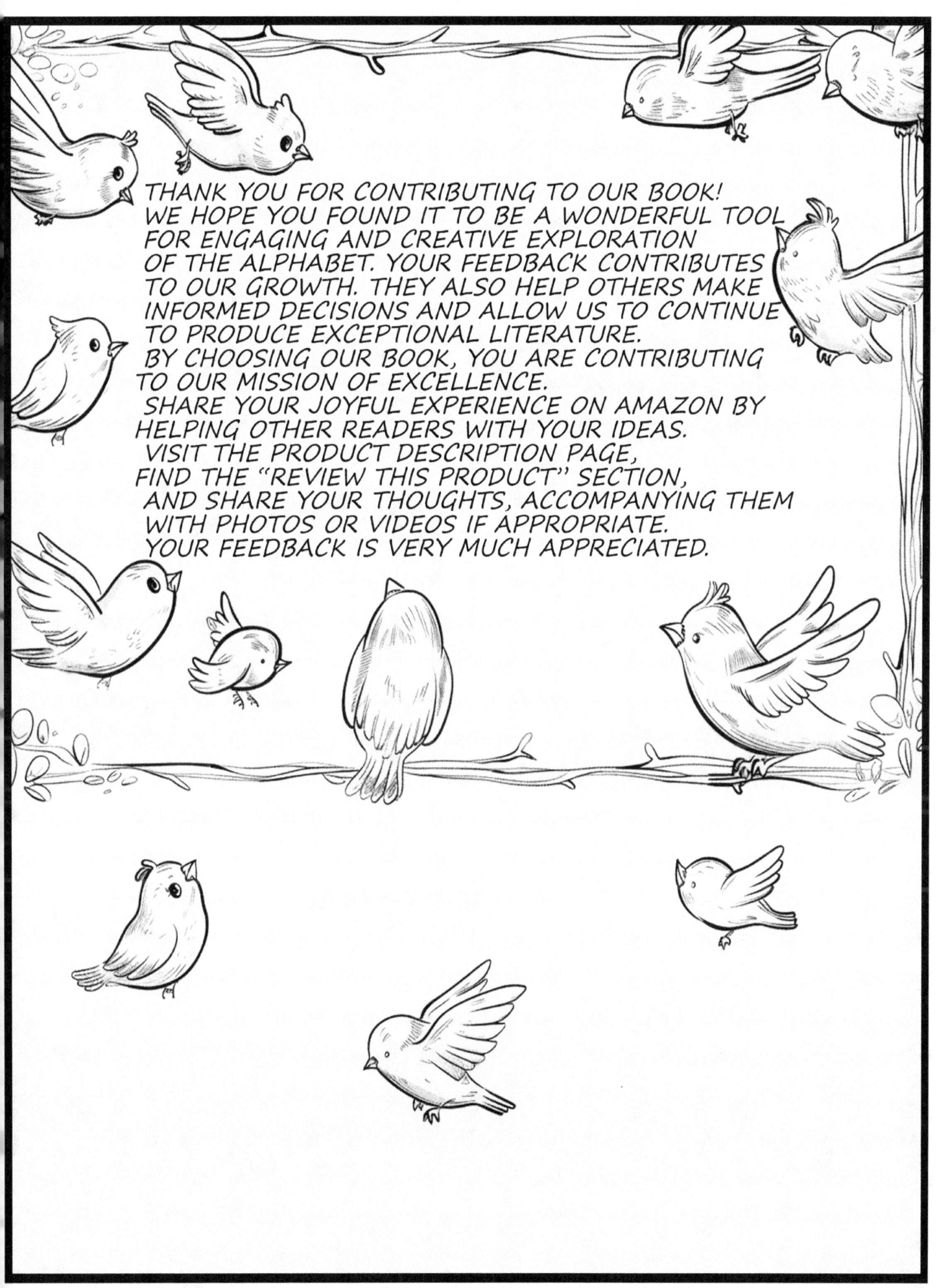

www.ingramcontent.com/pod-product-compliance
Lightning Source LLC
Chambersburg PA
CBHW082341220526
45470CB00008B/2599